A MODEST PROPOSAL
AND OTHER SATIRES

Jonathan Swift

AUTHORED by Cora Frazier
UPDATED AND REVISED by Adam Kissel

COVER DESIGN by Table XI Partners LLC
COVER PHOTO by Olivia Verma and © 2005 GradeSaver, LLC

BOOK DESIGN by Table XI Partners LLC

Published by GradeSaver LLC, www.gradesaver.com

First published in the United States of America by GradeSaver LLC. 2010

GRADESAVER, the GradeSaver logo and the phrase "Getting you the grade since 1999" are registered trademarks of GradeSaver, LLC

ISBN 978-1-60259-214-8

Printed in the United States of America

For other products and additional information please visit
http://www.gradesaver.com

Table of Contents

Table of Contents

Biography of Swift, Jonathan (1667-1745)

Jonathan Swift was an author, journalist, and political activist best known for his satirical novel *Gulliver's Travels* and for his satirical essay on the Irish famine, "A Modest Proposal."

Born of English parents in Dublin, Ireland, Swift studied at Kilkenny Grammar School and at Trinity College in Dublin. The abdication of King James II drove him to England. During his time in England, Swift realized his great talent for satire and wrote *A Tale of a Tub* and "The Battle of the Books," published in 1704. Swift also decided upon a career in the clergy. When he returned to Ireland, Swift became a member of the Anglican clergy, ordained in the Church of Ireland.

During the reign of Queen Anne (1702-14), Swift visited London several times, making a name for himself as a talented essayist. He began his political career as a part of the Whig political party but in 1710 switched sides, becoming a Tory and taking over the Tory journal *The Examiner*. Swift was disgusted by the Whigs' aversion to the Anglican Church and could not stand for the party's desire to do away with the Test Act, which kept many non-Anglicans from holding offices in government. Swift focused his time as a Tory on supporting their cause by writing lengthy pamphlets and essays on religion and politics, continuing to satirize those with different views. In 1713 Swift was offered the deanship of St. Patrick's Cathedral in Dublin. When Queen Anne died in 1714, the Tories came under fire, so Swift lost favor in London and greater England. He begrudgingly resigned himself to living full-time in Ireland.

In 1724 Swift led the Irish people in their resistance against the English, who continued to oppress them. He wrote many public letters and political pieces with the purpose of rallying the people. One of his most famous essays, "A Modest Proposal," satirically suggests that the Irish solve their problems of starvation and overpopulation by eating their young. Swift also engaged in extensive commentary on religion, though these works are not much read today. Even though Swift's identity was widely known by the citizens of Dublin, no one came forward to report him when a 300-pound reward was offered for his arrest.

Swift is also known for *Gulliver's Travels*, a book of fantasy, satire, and political allegory, much like his other, shorter works. He wrote *Gulliver's Travels* in 1725, and it was published in 1726. The book was a great success throughout the British Empire, and it contributed to Swift's fame and legitimacy as a writer and social commentator.

For the majority of his life, Swift was a victim of Meniere's disease, which affects balance and hearing and causes nausea and dizziness. When Swift was about 72 years old, his disease began to keep him from his duties and social life. He became withdrawn and deeply depressed. Swift died in October 1745. He was buried in St.

Patrick's Cathedral, where he had worked as dean.

Swift was a great friend of Alexander Pope, a fellow satirist best known for "Rape of the Lock." In a letter to Pope, Swift once called himself a misanthrope, but it seems more likely that he was simply frustrated by people who chose not to use the logic and reason they possessed.

About A Modest Proposal and Other Satires

A Modest Proposal and Other Satires is a collection of satirical works of political, social, and religious commentary by Jonathan Swift. The most famous of his essays—perhaps the most famous essay of satire in the English language—is "A Modest Proposal for Preventing the Children of Poor People in Ireland from Being a Burden to Their Parents of Country; and for Making Them Beneficial to the Public." This essay was published anonymously in 1729, a year in which Ireland suffered from poverty and famine. "A Modest Proposal" suggests, as a method for dealing with the destitution, that the Irish eat their babies.

Swift, of course, was not serious. His essay exposed the prejudice against the Irish poor by taking that prejudice to an extreme with a shocking suggestion. Swift also intended to lampoon a series of proposals that were being published at the time about solving Ireland's economic problems, although many of them were unfeasible and unhelpful. By asserting, like these other pamphlets, to have a cure-all solution, Swift exposed the naiveté of such a view. "A Modest Proposal" was also satirizing the new trend in political thought that applied scientific innovations to political questions. Many British thinkers of the day, including economist Sir William Petty (1623-1687), believed that simple mathematics was all it took to solve society's ills. Swift intended to mock this idea with "A Modest Proposal," suggesting that it isn't merely numbers, but people's lives that are at stake in political and social decisions.

This collection also contains other satirical works, mostly surrounding religious themes. *A Tale of a Tub* was published in 1704 and contributed to the Church of England's displeasure with Swift. The tale mocked the three main branches of Western Christianity, using a character to represent each branch, and generally mocked religious fervor and pride. "The Battle of the Books" was written as a companion to *Tale of a Tub*, and it takes place at the King's Library, which contained the British Royal Collection. In the battle, the books form two sides, the Ancients and the Moderns, and they literally fight one another in the library. "An Argument against Abolishing Christianity" was written around 1708 in response to attempts to repeal the Test Act of 1673, which required that individuals wishing to hold public positions take Communion with the Church of England. The Whigs wished to repeal this act, but Swift did not. "An Argument against Abolishing Christianity" exposes the dangers facing the Church from the arguments of Freethinkers.

"A True and Faithful Narrative of what passed in London during the General Consternation of All Ranks and Degrees of Mankind, on Tuesday, Wednesday, Thursday, and Friday Last" (1732) is likewise a parody of religious excess. "A True and Faithful Narrative" describes the lengths to which individuals go when they believe that a comet is about to strike, only to revert to their usual licentious behavior when this cataclysm does not occur. "A Meditation upon a Broomstick" (1710) was written in response to Robert Boyle's *Occasional Reflections upon Several Subjects* of 1655. Swift parodied Boyle--and so many others who met Swift's biting wit--for his writing style and Puritan beliefs.

Character List

The Father

In *A Tale of a Tub*, the man the story begins with in Section 2, the father of the three sons, who represents God. The coats he gives to them represent their respective Bibles.

Peter

Named for St. Peter, he represents Roman Catholicism in *A Tale of a Tub*.

Martin

Named for Protestant reformer Martin Luther, he represents the Church of England in *A Tale of a Tub*.

Jack

Named for John Calvin, he represents the dissenting Protestant denominations in *A Tale of a Tub*.

The Spider

He represents the faction of Moderns in "The Battle of the Books."

The Bee

The Bee represents the faction of Ancients in "The Battle of the Books."

"A Very Knowing American"

This is the man who tells the narrator of "A Modest Proposal" that infant flesh is delicious. He later assures the narrator that the flesh of fourteen-year-olds is too tough for consumption.

"A Very Worthy Person"

The man in "A Modest Proposal" who suggests to the narrator that the Irish also consume children of fourteen, as he has heard from the writer George Psalmanazar.

Mr. Whiston

The character who, in "A True and Faithful Narrative," deviates from his planned lecture to make a prediction that a comet will strike the earth.

Major Themes

Economic Inequality

Swift's persona highlights the economic inequality in Ireland and England with "A Modest Proposal." In the beginning of the essay, he expresses great sympathy for the beggars of Ireland, describing their destitution in detail. His solution of eating babies applies primarily to the babies of the poor; the title of the piece states that this is a proposal for making the "children of poor people" ultimately "beneficial to the public." The writer suggests that the landlords ought to eat the babies, as they have already "devoured" their parents. The writer here is implying that the rich metaphorically "devour" the poor, achieving success largely at the expense of the lower classes. The writer states in his final paragraph that his intention is not only to "relieve the poor" but also to "give pleasure to the rich." Swift's other satires, too, mock the rich. "An Argument Against the Abolishing of Christianity," for example, is narrated by a somewhat foppish narrator in order to expose the frivolities of the wealthy.

Cultural Arrogance and Colonialism

The narrator of "A Modest Proposal" is English, but he is making prescriptions for the Irish. With this structure, Swift reveals the cultural arrogance of the English and the political subjugation felt by the Irish. Swift mocks the view of the English as civilized and the Irish as an uncivilized "barbaric" or "savage" people. Rumors had been circulating in the eighteenth century about cannibalism among such "inferior" groups as the Irish and Native Americans. Claims like these were used to support England's right to rule over these peoples and colonize new territories. Swift has an American suggest cannibalism in "A Modest Proposal," as Americans (especially Native Americans) were seen as a savage, culturally inferior group compared to the English.

Religious Satire

Almost every satirical work in this collection deals with the matter of religious excess in some form, especially *A Tale of a Tub* and "A True and Faithful Narrative." *A Tale of a Tub* portrays three brothers, who represent the three branches of Western Christianity, as all naturally licentious and without true religious conviction, having only outward appearances of conviction. "A Faithful Narrative," too, portrays a largely sinful town thrown into displays of repentance when the people believe a comet is coming. "A Modest Proposal" mocks anti-Catholic religious prejudice, as the narrator calls the Irish babies "papists" because they are Catholic.

Satire of Literary Style

Swift's satires do not merely comment upon certain political, social, or religious beliefs; they are also commentary about how those beliefs are expressed. Swift's satire is always also literary satire. Swift wrote "A Meditation Upon A Broomstick" to mock not only Robert Boyle's Puritanism but also Boyle's writing style itself, calling Boyle a "silly writer." "A Modest Proposal," too, sought to mock the "can-do" attitude of many writers of the day, who thought that only one simple solution was needed to cure large and complex problems. In addition, Swift's use of flowery language to suggest strange or wild things generally serves to mock the use of such language.

Ancients vs. Moderns

"The Battle of the Books" begins with a quarrel between two factions, the Ancients and the Moderns, and soon spirals into literal combat between the groups of books. The Ancients represent the literary classics of ancient Greece and to some extent Rome, characterized by investigation into the nature of things, for instance as espoused by Swift's contemporary and good friend Alexander Pope in his satirical poems. Moderns who appreciate the Ancients and do not merely go off in new directions also can be said to be on the side of the Ancients. The Modern faction represents newer, scientific, reason-centered Enlightenment thought based more in theorizing than in reality, and with a strong sense of self-reliance. The factions, respectively, are figured as a bee and a spider.

Family

Family is a theme in both *A Tale of a Tub* and "A Modest Proposal." In *A Tale of a Tub*, the father of the three brothers, when he gives them their respective coats, requests that they always live together as brethren. This is an allegory for the ecumenical Christian "family" of one Church, despite doctrinal differences. The suggestion is that Christians, although of different specific beliefs, are "brothers" and should act as such. In "A Modest Proposal," too, family is a theme with broader implications; in this instance the larger "family" is that of the Irish people, which Swift's narrator offensively calls a "breed." The narrator says that poor parents will support his proposal because it would relieve them of the burden of caring for their young. Swift's narrator suggests that family is nothing to the Irish, exposing British prejudices yet reinforcing the idea of communal Irish struggle.

The Moral Dangers of Scientific Advancement

"A Modest Proposal" hints at the dangers of certain types of new knowledge. At the time Swift was writing, many political thinkers had started to apply new theories of science and mathematics to their social ideas. Swift parodies this view by dedicating a few paragraphs of "A Modest Proposal" to calculating the number of babies available for consumption. By doing so, he demonstrates the perils of seeing things only in terms of numbers. Swift suggests that this new kind of social math leaves no room for humanity; people are not numbers. With the calculations present in "A Modest Proposal" Swift expresses his unease with taking reason and scientific advancement too far and forgetting the human side of policy. The bee and the Ancients similarly criticize the spider and the Moderns in "The Battle of the Books."

Glossary of Terms

Anabaptists

radical Protestants who rejected infant baptism because they thought only an active believer should be baptized; they emphasized free will. They historically have been considered to emphasize justification by works in addition to faith, but critics argue that this idea was circulated falsely out of misunderstanding or in order to discredit them.

arbiter

judge

besom

a broom made of twigs and a longer handle; a cleansing or sweeping-away force

commonplace-books

collections of interesting facts learned by reading or conversation; in the absence of the Internet, these were especially popular in Early Modern times, as people would write down meaningful lines and know where to find them

coxcomb

a fop; a vain and foolish person

deplorable

lamentable; worthy of harsh censure

dignities

the upper class of society

Dissenters

Protestants who separated themselves from the Church of England because they disliked the bishop structure and entanglement with government

emulation

imitation, often out of admiration

expedient

a solution or a means to an end

farrow

to give birth

fricassee
stewed dish often made with chicken

groat
a small-denomination British coin that has been discontinued

halfporth
a shortened form of "halfpennyworth," a small amount of money

Jacobites
those who wanted the monarchy, in the form of the Stuart line, to be reinstated in Britain, and rejected the Revolution Settlement of 1689

papist
an offensive term for a Roman Catholic

paradox of the moderns
the Moderns, having returned to classical themes, are more ancient than the Ancients

periwig
the original word for wig; primarily an eighteenth-century fashion worn by both men and women, often powdered, and partly because people often shaved their heads to avoid lice

play
gambling

Privy Council
In England, a body responsible for declaring war and other administrative duties; in Ireland, a group primarily of bishops responsible for law-making. The Irish Privy Council had to first submit its proposals to the English Privy Council.

prodigious
marvelously great; inducing wonder

ragout
thick, well-seasoned stew served as a main dish

rudiments
basic principles or elements

scrupulous

careful, exacting, complying with strict morals

Scythians

an ancient eastern European and Asiatic Russian people, often nomadic, sometimes considered barbarians, who were often compared to the Irish for their supposed savagery

tenet

belief or principle; a component of a larger doctrine

Test Act

a law passed in England in 1673 that required potential office holders to take communion with the Church of England, which would demonstrate Anglicanism

viceroy

a governor, in Ireland called the Lord-Lieutenant

vintner

wine merchant

Whigs

a political party formed in 1679 whose members strongly supported the Resolution Settlement of 1689, believed in quelling domestic Catholic threats, and disapproved of monarchy

Glossary of Terms

Short Summary

A Modest Proposal and Other Satires contains six satirical pieces, the most famous being "A Modest Proposal," in which Swift ironically suggests that the people of Ireland should eat their young.

A Tale of A Tub, a religious satire, is the longest piece in the work; not only does Swift parody the three Western branches of Christianity (their history, their excesses their hypocrisy), but he also parodies trends in literary, philosophical, and medical thought. A father, representing God, has three sons, each representing one of the branches. They work hard to reinterpret their father's will in order to get the results they want as they spruce up their coats, until finally it is time for reform and the difficult task of undoing the baubles caught up in the coats.

"The Battle of the Books" is an extended allegory of the intellectual and poetic battles between the Ancients and the Moderns, with send-ups of many of Swift's contemporaries as pitifully weak compared with ancient writers. The Ancients definitely have most of the advantages, but some Moderns do fairly well, particularly those who make best use of the enduring value of ancient writings. The story, which reads a lot like Homer's *Iliad*, ends unfinished, with two of the modern critics stabbed to death.

"An Argument Against the Abolishing of Christianity" and "A True and Faithful Narrative" have religious themes. The former examines and rejects several arguments that have been put forth for abolishing Christianity, and explains the disadvantages of getting rid of it in England. The latter is a fairly straightforward tale about religious hypocrisy. There is a prophecy that a comet will strike; the people temporarily reform and come clean about their sins; the comet fails to strike and the people return to their old ways.

"A Meditation Upon a Broomstick" is almost entirely a literary parody. It turns out that man is very like a broomstick, often being upside-down and irrational, sweeping up and raking up dirt as people criticize one another, and becoming soiled in the process.

"A Modest Proposal" purports to address the problems of poverty and overpopulation in Ireland with a simple economic solution: the Irish should eat their babies when the infants become one year old. While some serious alternatives are provided, the piece at least involves a humorous method of getting people thinking about the real issues and how they might be solved in a way other than cannibalism.

Quotes and Analysis

"I am assured by a very knowing American of my acquaintance in London; that a young healthy child, well nursed, is, at a year old, a most delicious, nourishing, and wholesome food; whether stewed, roasted, baked or boiled, and I make no doubt, that it will equally serve in a fricassee, or ragout."

"A Modest Proposal," p. 207

This is perhaps the most famous line in the essay. It is in this sentence that Swift grounds the gastronomical side of his satirical "modest proposal" that the people of Ireland should eat their young. Swift introduces this idea in the most shocking way possible with his claim that one-year-old babies are "delicious" whether they are "stewed, roasted, baked or boiled." The image of a baby in a fricassee or a ragout is equally horrifying and absurd. The idea is so extreme that it demonstrates the overall irony of the piece. It is also worth noting that this line comes late in the essay. Swift lulls the reader into a false sense of trust in the narrator's good intentions by beginning with descriptions of the position of the poor in Ireland. The reader may think at first that this is a serious essay, making the point all the more jarring when it eventually appears. The idea itself comes from "a very knowing American," suggesting something of the wild barbarism of the Americas and American colonies.

"For first, as I have already observed, it would greatly lessen the number of papists, with whom we are yearly overrun, being the principal breeders of the nation as well as our dangerous enemies ..."

"A Modest Proposal," p. 210

The plain argument is that if the Irish children are eaten, there will be fewer Irish Catholics to contend with. This line is emblematic of the religious prejudices Swift intended to expose with "A Modest Proposal." The "papists" are Catholics, those who believe in the spiritual primacy of the Pope. Swift is writing in the voice of an extreme, bigoted English Protestant in order to mock such a person. He reveals the stereotype that the Irish have lots of children by having his narrator call them "the principal breeders." Swift's narrator also asserts that the Irish Catholics are "our dangerous enemies." Swift was not suggesting that he believed any of these things. He more likely was suggesting that such beliefs were destructive and foolish, since he put those ideas in the writing of a very prejudiced narrator.

"I can think of no one objection that will possibly be raised against this proposal, unless it should be urged that the number of people will be thereby much lessened in the kingdom."

"A Modest Proposal," p. 212

This line, late in "A Modest Proposal," heightens the piece's overall satirical effect. Up to this point, the satire has derived chiefly from the absurd proposals. When the reader encounters the "unless," the reader might think that the writer is about to acknowledge that, after all, the idea of eating babies is morally wrong. Swift subverts this expectation by continuing the satire, naming the unexpected objection of mere population depletion. Although the Irish are the enemy and it is better to have few of them, at least they help develop the economy and the countryside. With this added irony, Swift is further heightening the satire, suggesting that the writer does not even conceive that the idea of killing and eating Irish one-year-olds could be morally wrong.

"A very worthy person, a true lover of his country, and whose virtues I highly esteem, was lately pleased in discoursing on this matter to offer a refinement upon my scheme."

"A Modest Proposal," p. 208

The writer suggests that he is not the only one prejudiced enough to support such an idea as eating Irish children. It is "a very worthy person" who truly loves England who agrees with him and even has offered to improve the narrator's original idea. This "worthy person" is supposedly a modern thinker of the English upper class. The person suggests eating the flesh of fourteen-year-old children in addition to infants, which would reduce a child-bearing Irish generation as well. Thus the satire is extended to an entire class of Englishmen.

This quarrel first began, as I have heard it affirmed by an old dweller in the neighbourhood, about a small spot of ground, lying and being upon one of the two tops of the hill Parnassus; the highest and largest of which had, it seems, been time out of mind in quiet possession of certain tenants, called the Ancients; and the other was held by the Moderns.

"The Battle of the Books," p. 161

This line sets up the "Ancients" and "Moderns" dichotomy, which later was attributed to Swift and reformulated by other writers such as Leo Strauss. Here, these are the two sides in the literal "battle" which commences among the books of the British Royal Library. According to the "old dweller," the argument began when the Moderns, occupying the lower place on the Parnassus, grew jealous of the Ancients, who were on the higher peak.

"As when a skilful cook has trussed a brace of woodcocks, he with iron skewer pierces the tender sides of both, their legs and wings close pinioned to the ribs; joined in their lives, joined in their deaths; so closely joined that Charon would mistake them both for one, and waft them over Styx for half his fare."

Quotes and Analysis

This line is at the climactic conclusion of the "battle" as recorded, though the battle continues. Boyle, on the side of the ancients, stabs Bentley and Wotton, who are on the side of the moderns, and the two friends are so close together (being speared together) that they seem as one. This is most likely because both authors appeared literally in the same book, bound together. In "The Bookseller to the Reader," the introductory material to "Battle of the Books," it is remarked, "The controversy [between Ancients and Moderns] took its rise from an essay of Sir William Temple's upon that subject; which was answered by W. Wotton, B.D., with an appendix by Dr. Bentley." As for Charon, one had to pay him a toll to be ferried across the River Styx, which is how dead people got to the Underworld, which is where these friends would be headed if they were not actually books. Giving the two friends the demeaning "woodcock" imagery suggests that Swift is on the side of Boyle and the Ancients, but since we do not know the conclusion of the battle, Swift might be making only the more limited point that Boyle may have had the better argument, for now, against the other two writers.

"However, I know not how, whether from the affectation of singularity, or the perverseness of human nature, but so it unhappily falls out, that I cannot be entirely of this opinion [that we ought to abolish Christianity]."
"An Argument Against the Abolition of Christianity," p. 189

This is another good example of satire. Swift suggests that it may be "affectation" or perversity that causes him to want to keep Christianity from being abolished. At the time he was writing, abolishing the religion would have been absurd. This is about as absurd as the idea about eating babies from "A Modest Proposal." It is extreme and shocking to imagine Christianity being abolished in that culture, but it is especially shocking to imagine a situation in which to being opposed to abolishing Christianity would make a person "perverse." As in "A Modest Proposal," Swift is taking certain ideas to the extreme for effect. He hopes, with this line, and with this piece, to liken the abolishing of Christianity to the repeal of the Test Act of 1673, which required individuals who wished to hold public office to take Communion. He wants to mock those who wish to repeal the Test Act, suggesting that doing away with a test of proper religious faith (Anglicanism) would be like repealing Christianity itself.

"Once upon a time there was a man who had three sons by one wife, and all at birth, neither could the midwife tell certainly which was the eldest."
"A Tale of a Tub," p. 56

In Section 2 of "The Tale of a Tub," Swift is introducing the three brothers who will represent the three forms of Western Christianity: Catholicism, The Church of

England, and Protestant Dissenters. The father represents God. Swift writes that the midwife could not tell "which was the eldest," implying that it is difficult to discern which form of Christianity maintains the original Christian tradition. This plot element recalls the situation in Genesis when two twins are born at the same time in such a way that it is impossible to say with certainty which twin is older. Also, "Once upon a time" immediately establishes this text as a kind of allegorical fairy tale.

"But a broomstick, perhaps you will say, is an emblem of a tree standing on its head; and pray what is man, but a topsy-turvy creature, his animal faculties perpetually mounted on his rational, his head where his heels should be, grovelling on the earth! and yet, with all his faults, he sets up to be a universal reformer and corrector of abuses, a remover of grievances, rakes into every slut's corner of nature, bringing hidden corruption to the light, and raises a mighty dust where there was none before, sharing deeply all the while in the very same pollutions he pretends to sweep away."

"A Meditation Upon a Broomstick," p. 232

This passage is from a very short parody of Robert Boyle's *Occasional Reflections Upon Several Subjects*. Swift is mocking Boyle's literary style, with its almost stream-of-consciousness reflections that seem to go almost nowhere. This satirical passage exposes what Swift truly thought about Boyle: that he was a "silly writer," characteristically writing silly reflections like this. The serious point in the passage as written is that people often set themselves up as moral judges, nosing into other people's dirty laundry, which means getting their own noses dirty, not unlike what happens to a broom when it is used to sweep away the dust. To really investigate the gutter, one must put part of oneself in the gutter. "Rakes into every slut's corner" seems like an intentionally bawdy double entendre; a "rake" is an immoral man as well as a device used to stir up a fire. A "slut" could be any untidy or dirty woman, or a maid; the word has roots in the idea of being muddy.

"All the quality and gentry were perfectly ashamed, nay, some utterly disowned that they had manifested any signs of religion."

"A True and Faithful Narrative," p. 227

Here, Swift is mocking religious excess and hypocrisy. In "A True and Faithful Narrative," when Mr. Whiston makes the prediction that a comet will strike the earth, the town goes into a frenzy of repentance and religious extremes. When the comet fails to strike, they return to their old ways, as this line illustrates. Swift is suggesting that none of this religious feeling was genuine.

Quotes and Analysis

Summary and Analysis of Front Matter to "A Tale of a Tub"

A Tale of a Tub today begins with an "Apology" defending it against those who argued that it was an immoral book. (The Apology was added in 1710.) The author responds that he used satire to expose the follies of religion and learning. If a person wrote a treatise about the flaws in law or physics, lawyers and students of physics would be grateful, not angry. The author also defends the book against charges of plagiarism, acknowledging only minimal borrowing from others, and arguing that the work is original. The writer also relates the problems he encountered publishing the book; the incomplete nature of the final product is due in part to a publishing mistake, not an oversight. The postscript to the apology condemns a recently published *Notes on the Tale of a Tub*, which he says is a misinterpretation.

At one time the text began with an "Advert" or advertisement, identifying "treatises written by the same author, including such items as "A Panegyrical Essay upon the Number THREE," "A General History of Ears," and similarly odd works.

Next comes a letter to the Right Honourable John Lord Sommers from the bookseller, in which the bookseller offers to dedicate the piece to Sommers, which would help the book sell. He noticed the words "DETUR DIGNISSIMO" on the present book but did not know Latin, and neither did the authors he worked with, so he got the Curate of the Parish to translate it: "Let it be given to the worthiest." The Curate also told him that it meant the book should be dedicated "to the sublimest genius of the age." The bookseller went around to different "wits" he knew, asking them who it could refer to, and they all said it seemed directed at themselves or, at least, Sommers.

The bookseller has examined one or two hundred dedications in order to write one here. He also asked the wits for advice, and they brought back a huge list of virtues for him to use, though the words seemed like nothing extraordinary, and it was a waste of money to get their help. Others, however, examined the list, or at least the first few lines, and determined that the list fit Sommers uniquely. It would be more interesting to find that Sommers had done something brave or at least fashionable, but it is not so interesting just to discuss virtues like eloquence, wisdom, and justice. There are many virtues to mention, but it seems that historians do not believe in the truth of lists of virtues put in dedications, so this is another reason not to go into detail. A final reason is that Sommers may have already exerted too much patience to keep reading.

Next, a letter from the bookseller to the reader explains that the bookseller is publishing this without the author's permission, six years after receiving the manuscript. The author had given it up for lost, and the bookseller will not reveal what happened. It seems that another, altered version of this text has already appeared, so the bookseller is bringing out "the whole work in its naturals." But it is too hard for the bookseller to understand, and it would be helpful to have a "key" to unlock "the more difficult parts."

Next is "The Epistle Dedicatory to his Royal Highness Prince Posterity," dated December 1697, in which the author provides the actual dedication to the book. The author made good use of leisure time, such as rainy days, to write the book. Posterity has important virtues, given that the future is the "sole arbiter of the productions of human wit in this polite and most accomplished age." Posterity seems to have little regard for most of what has been written lately, which is generally true of any plethora of present writers. Most works fade away—and quickly. For instance, of the best 136 contemporary poets, it seems that none will last. All of this is due to posterity's "governor," fate. As another example, many works whose authors thought were great, hours later are gone and replaced with more writings, withering away as fast as fashion and the news.

The best names the author can offer as poets or writers are people whose writings are nevertheless hard to find, like John Dryden, for his translation of Virgil; Nahum Tate; Tom Durfey; critics Rymer and Dennis; and Dr. Bentley with his "yoke-mate" William Wotton (whose writings have been published bound together).

Finally, the Preface to *A Tale of a Tub* begins with an explanation of the point of this exercise. As the metaphor goes, the Ship of State (and of the Church) is in danger of being critiqued by various writers. The writers tend to draw their critique from Hobbes' *Leviathan* which, like a whale, is formidable indeed. Just as seamen can distract a whale by giving it something amusing to play with—an empty tub—it has been proposed to give these writers a bunch of vapid "schemes of religion and government" to think about and write about, diverting them from critiquing the actual Church and State. The present work is intended to similarly distract these writers: "it was decreed that, in order to prevent these Leviathans from tossing and sporting with the commonwealth, which of itself is too apt to fluctuate, they should be diverted from that game by 'A Tale of a Tub.'" The long-term solution is to corral these critics into a new Academy where they will not do much damage. Meanwhile, this tale should provide plenty of grist for the mill.

He also discusses the nature of introductions and prefaces in general. Writers waste a lot of words complaining about people wasting words, and go on to waste more. Perhaps once a book is written, there is nothing left to think or write. Also, writing wit for the moment is a very delicate, fleeting, contingent business. The author argues that to really understand a writer's work, one should put oneself in the milieu of the writer at the time of writing. Thus, one should realize that the present writer conceived of his ideas "in bed in a garret" and in illness and poverty.

He adds that there is not "one grain of satire intermixed" with this discourse. Satirists just slap the rears of the public, which has little effect; they are like weeds or broken razors. "Besides," he writes, "those whose teeth are too rotten to bite are best of all others qualified to revenge that defect with their breath." Yet, satires are easier to come up with than panegyrics, since there are but few virtues and many vices. Also, in England, people are praised for denigrating the morals of the people, so long as nobody important is personally named.

Analysis

All of this material in *A Tale of a Tub* is introductory; the actual tale has not yet begun. Nevertheless we here meet the most important character, the author, not to be confused with Swift himself, except perhaps in the Apology. We also meet the bookseller and, through him, some of the people who have interacted with the bookseller.

The "Apology for the, &c." appears to be a rare moment of candor, as Swift is claiming to speak in his own voice directly to the reader. Knowing that he is a great satirist, however, we must continue to be skeptical. Swift claims that the poor reception of *A Tale of a Tub* has bothered him; he appears genuinely upset by bad reviews. His tone suggests wounded pride and arrogance, deriding those who might think that his work is immoral. Swift writes that he "wrote only to the men of wit and taste" (p. 21). That is, this was a book not for the common man but for an elite. His tone is also defensively self-serving in the declaration that his work is uniquely his own when he argues, "it was never disputed to be an original" (p. 16). Yet, this self-importance is very close to what the author satirizes about other writers later in the introductory material. It may well be that Swift found a way to defend himself and at the same time acknowledge his own vanity.

The discussion of the publishing mistake suggests that all of this is satire after all, even though the points should be taken with some seriousness. After all, satire is often meant to offend, but indirectly. The hilarious "Advert" indirectly offends all such writers who think they are important enough to write significant works about the number three or the history of ears.

The letter dedicated to Lord Sommers is of course not really a letter from the bookseller; Swift is poking fun at those who may misunderstand his treatise, which he is doing throughout his work. Swift signals that he knows his book will not be understood; he expects it. He appeals to the pride of the reader by repeating the idea in the "Apology" that this book is only for "the worthiest" of men. While in Plato's work "The Apology of Socrates," where Socrates is said to go around to different citizens proving how ignorant they are despite their thinking that they are smart, the bookseller is an unwitting Socrates, proving the same point without even knowing it. That is, he shows how vain everyone is when they think that "the worthiest" most likely refers to them. There is a much deeper lesson here; this very work of Swift's is indeed only for a small elite, the true "worthiest," who will understand Swift's jokes, see the satire for what it is, and learn what Swift has to teach about religion, which is a very difficult subject to treat head-on, since it is politically dangerous to criticize religion, especially during Swift's era around 1700.

Yet, if you think yourself so smart that you are in the elite, chances are good that you are like the others, thinking you are wise when you really are not. At the least, superficial readers are going to give up if they try to read the dense prose and winding sentences. Reading this work takes a lot of work, and if you find yourself skipping sentences or paragraphs because they just seem too confusing, this work is perhaps not meant for you, or at least not yet. If you do find yourself getting the jokes, you are becoming well prepared to read the main tale.

Meanwhile, the bookseller's lengthy praise of Lord Sommers serves Sommers' alleged vanity, satirizing the common sycophantic praise that one often finds at the beginning of books, as well as the stroking praise that the lower class generally offers to the upper classes, which is a common theme for Swift.

The letter from the bookseller to the reader is likewise a parody of booksellers. The bookseller says he worked on the manuscript a bit himself, not respecting the author's intentions. This must have been a wildly hopeless task, given how profoundly he fails to understand the work. He only published it because someone else published some form of it first, and he did not want to lose out on possible profits.

The author assumes a properly submissive tone in the letter to "prince posterity," calling him "your highness" and other grand monikers. It was something of a tradition to write letters such as these before the publication of a work that one knew would be controversial in one's own time, but not necessarily controversial in the judgment of a future, more enlightened age. Yet, many people who think they are too good for their time are quite wrong, and once again the message is to be humble about one's true worth as a writer or as a reader.

The Preface to *A Tale of a Tub* finally gets to explaining the work's title. Just like sailors distract a whale by throwing a tub into the water, this author is distracting the various readers who might otherwise trouble the Church and the State. Instead of giving them the deep critiques that could really do harm, this work gives them an extended allegory that will keep them occupied trying to figure out which details refer to which realities about the religions. In a sense, it is suggested, this is also what a good university might do, keeping the smart but impractical people away from government!

The "Introduction" satirizes introductions. The introductions never seem to end, as Section One is also an introduction. With this structure, Swift mocks the high-handedness of certain authors who pen elaborate prefaces describing what they intend to write--instead of devoting time to what they are actually writing.

Overall, Swift offers that a really good piece of writing is a hard nut to crack; one cannot understand a piece merely as a superficial reader. On the one hand, many writers write long, winding, impenetrable introductions, thinking they are being profound. On the other hand, Swift's introduction is long, winding, and nearly impenetrable, parodying the others, yet Swift is doing his best to say something profound. If nothing else, he demonstrates the folly of mankind and saves us the time of putting up with the huge cloud of second-rate writers. Swift masterfully satirizes a style at the same time that he uses that style productively.

Summary and Analysis of "A Tale of a Tub," Sections 1-10

Section One, the "Introduction," begins with a discussion of the ways that writers rise above the crowd and make their thoughts known, including the pulpit, the ladder (or place for making lectures), and the stage itinerant (which at the time could also refer to the gallows). It proceeds to satirize introductions, pointing out, for instance, that a good writer is said to hide his best points rather than state them plainly, like hiding a nut inside a shell. (Meanwhile, this is exactly what Swift is doing, at length.) He finally introduces his treatise proper, noting an original intention to split it into forty sections.

Section Two begins with a man speaking to his three sons, Peter, Jack and Martin, before his death. He is bequeathing to them very special coats, which will never wear and which will always fit. He gives his sons instructions for caring well for his coats. The sons travel for seven years and take good care of their coats. Then, they meet three women, with whom they fall in love, and they proceed to commit all kinds of sins. The three brothers want to put shoulder-knots onto their coats (shoulder-knots being in fashion) but, since there is nothing explicit in their father's will about shoulder-knots, they instead look for the mere letters in the word "shoulder-knots" in their father's will. Upon finding those letters, or close to those letters, they are satisfied that such an alteration is acceptable. The brothers continue to alter their coats, according to fashion trends, always finding some justification for the alteration within their father's will.

Section Three is the first official digression, "A Digression Concerning Critics." The three brothers' story is interrupted as the writer discusses the nature of criticism and makes a distinction between the "critic" and the "true critic." The latter has more natural instinct and is drawn to greater genius—liabilities rather than virtues, the reader suspects. He also discusses the difference between the Ancients and the Moderns, as well as Ancient and Modern ways of thought.

Section Four returns to his narrative about the brothers. Peter claims he is the eldest brother and therefore is due all sorts of titles and honors. He embarks on several projects: buying a continent, devising new remedies, erecting a "whispering-house," creating an office of insurance, supporting street shows, inventing a new kind of pickle, breeding a new kind of bull, and handing out pardons to criminals. Peter becomes rich and has delusions about his self-importance. His brothers try to intervene, but they realize that they are unable to stop his fits of madness, and they leave him. They revisit their father's will, translating it into common speech, and they come to a new understanding of what their father desired of them.

"A Digression in the Modern Kind" now begins by justifying the very act of digression. It argues that sometimes diversion is more instructive than instruction. This digression resumes the Ancients versus Moderns topic and criticizes Modern forms of thought.

Section Six returns to the brothers. Peter is still rich and comfortable, but his two brothers are destitute, and they live together for comfort. They return to their two coats and their father's will, trying to return entirely to their father's desires. They therefore begin to remove the adornments affixed to the coat. Martin does this slowly and carefully, while Jack, in his anger, removes the adornments all at once, tearing the coat. In this way, the brothers begin to grow apart.

"The Digression in Praise of Digressions" now discusses how certain types of argument can be illuminating, especially when running parallel to certain other types of argument. This digression then evaluates the modern wit, providing suggestions to the reader regarding how to appear witty.

Section Eight discusses the nature of wind and inspiration. The next section, "A Digression Concerning Madness," mentions Jack briefly because he is considered by the author to be mad. The author discusses the great men who have changed history, many of whom were of religious conviction, and proceeds to tell the story of several men who fit this description. He assesses what it was, mentally, that allowed them to achieve such heights. Madness here is a kind of "excess of vapors" that produces genius. The author suggests that society seek out those young men who appear disturbed and give them power, for it is likely that they possess this "madness" of greatness.

Section Ten begins with a remark that authors provide prefaces or introductions to all sorts of works, offering their thoughts grandly to the world. Thus, the author is doing the same, expressing a wish that his piece be well-received. The author lists different types of readers--the superficial, the ignorant, and the learned--and predicts how each kind reacts to satire. It is for the latter, the learned, that he writes. He then discusses the different types of interpretations that be gleaned from any text, and he offers some interpretations of his own text, noting, for example, that if a reader were to multiply the number of instances of the letter o by seven and then divide it by nine, he would uncover a great mystery.

Section Eleven offers a truism about the kinship of a traveler and his horse, especially when on a difficult journey in which obstacles (such as dogs) are encountered. Finally we return to the story of Jack, who has a very active imagination. Jack returns to his father's will in order to glean its meaning but, after a while, decides that such a meaning is "deeper" and "darker" than he first thought. He starts finding evidence in his father's will (which was only about the coats) for all sorts of actions he takes in life. Gradually, Jack begins to become more fanatical, playing tricks and having fits, disliking it when he might hear music or see color. Although they are sworn enemies, Jack and Peter keep running into one another in the city. The author complains about not being able to give more detail about the brothers, but he can summarize their most recent actions: Jack and Peter have teamed up against their brother Martin in order to serve their own agendas. Nevertheless,

Summary and Analysis of "A Tale of a Tub," Sections 1-10

when Peter gets into trouble, Jack abandons him, and vice versa.

The conclusion declares that a work that is too long is as damaging as a book that is too short, and that there is a time and place for every kind of book. The author describes the conversation with his bookseller that gave rise to this particular book, predicting that he will be an author for the ages. He also describes other authors of his acquaintance, and says that he has come to make many friends.

Analysis

The blank place in Section One is purposeful, although the author wrote earlier that he lost some of the pages; here, too, he is being satirical. The list of books he has read, with far from accurate descriptions of what those books are actually about, is likewise supposed to be funny; these are not books that one would choose for close examination, and it appears that the narrator has woefully misunderstood those books. This is a central theme: people misunderstand what they read, for a variety of reasons and with a variety of results ranging from the comic to the tragic.

The father in the beginning of the tale, when it finally begins in Section Two, represents God, and his sons the three Western branches of the Christian church. (See the character list for details.) The coats that he bequeaths them represent tradition, and his will, which the sons are supposed to interpret correctly and follow, is an allegory for Scripture. The women with whom the three brothers fall in love are meant to represent the sins of Covetousness, Ambition and Pride. (Duchess d'Argent is the Dame of Silver; Madame de Grands-Titres is the Madame of Great Titles, and the Countess d'Orgueil is the Countess of Pride.) The fact that the brothers so quickly fall in love with these sinful women and soon descend into sin themselves, is commentary on the fragility of religion in human hands. The discussion of the "idol" to whom sacrifices are made is an allegory for a tailor, and the "fashions" with which the brothers become so enamored represent trends in religious or philosophical thought, which cause religions to alter their original structure. When the brothers interpret their father's will in strange and ridiculous ways (such as looking for the presence of mere letters instead of actual words), Swift is satirizing the all-too-common habit of interpreting Scripture to justify whatever people would like to do.

"A Digression Concerning Critics" is literary parody. The writer mocks the language of criticism itself; the "true" critic is supposedly today's writer who merely sets himself up as a critic and lets his ideas flow. The reader must suspect that Swift really means that the best critics are the ones who the writer says are extinct—those who genuinely recover the best of the past and who genuinely assess what is good and bad in others' work. This section also suggests a dichotomy between Ancients and Moderns that he will expand upon elsewhere in "The Battle of the Books."

In Section Four, Peter's madness and richness are meant to represent the Catholic Church at its height; his projects such as "buying a new continent" and "erecting a whispering-house" are meant to represent the actions that the Catholic Church took to make admittance into Heaven easier ("buying a new continent," suggests the introduction of purgatory, and "erecting a new whispering-house" refers to an expansion of confession.) One section refers to the sale of "indulgences," which the author condemns because they seemed to let people off the hook after committing serious crimes, if they only gave the Church enough money. At the end of the section, the two brothers express the same criticism and get thrown out, which directly reflects the one of the Protestant criticisms of the Catholic Church at the time of the Reformation.

Swift's literary parody continues with "A Digression in the Modern Kind." This digression is, as one might now expect, a parody of literary digressions. His main purpose appears to be to parody the way certain philosophers write. For instance, he says ridiculously self-congratulatory things, such as: "I hold myself obliged to give as much light as is possible to into the beauties and excellencies of what I am writing" (p. 95).

In Section Six, when the brothers return to their father's will, this is a reference to Martin Luther's and John Calvin's belief in the "plain sense" of Scripture, and their work to strip Christianity of all the additional non-scriptural elements that Roman Catholicism had added to it, by going back to the original language and practices. Swift's decision to make Martin and Jack alter their coats differently is representative of how Calvinism was further dissenting from Catholicism than Lutheranism was; John Calvin took his reformation to a greater extreme than Martin Luther did. When Jack rips his coat, the suggestion is that Calvin went too far and ruined the religion by not carefully unfastening the embellishments. In contrast, Martin (Martin Luther) rips off the worst fringes but is careful not to damage the original coat, and even permits some of the embellishments to stay attached so as not to remove the good along with the bad.

In "A Digression in Praise of Digressions," Swift descends into literary parody again with his suggestions on how to be witty without having to actually read or think: one can simply learn the title or study the index.

Swift's discussion, in Section Eight, of wind as inspiring (humorously comparing wind to a "belch") is meant to suggest the nature of religious inspiration, which causes one to reinterpret Scripture or challenge the status quo. "A Digression Concerning Madness" is similarly separate from the main story; its separation, as well as the pieces missing from the text, highlight the very frantic "madness" about which Swift is writing; it is as though the writer himself is mad—unable to return to his main story, unable to present a complete text.

Swift's defense of madness, here, as not a malady but a mark of superior talent seems to be more sincere than usual. This is a rare moment in which it appears as if Swift actually believes the plain sense of the argument. His later descent into suggesting that young men who are strange or fitful be given command of great armies, however, indicates a return to satire. Section Ten's failure to return to the story of the three brothers likewise conforms structurally to Swift's idea of "madness"; the very arrangement of this tale seems mad.

In this section, Swift offers his work to the world in a high-handed way in order to parody those who write such long, self-congratulatory prefaces. His tone appears more earnest as he describes the different types of readers, but he then goes back into satire when he suggests methods of interpreting his work; the idea that the number of instances of the letter *o* might reveal any sort of mystery in the work is utterly ridiculous, and thus mocks such bizarre literary interpretations.

Swift continues to poke fun at the establishment of literature and learning with his conclusion which, although it has its moments serious in tone, is satirical in the description of Swift's conversation with his bookseller, describing with mock-drama how his bookseller "looked westward" before answering the question of what Swift ought to write. Likewise, with Swift's declaration that he will be remembered as an author, he parodies those men who have inflated ideas of their greatness.

Summary and Analysis of "The Battle of the Books"

"The Battle of the Books" begins with a note from the bookseller to the reader, telling the reader that it refers to a "famous dispute ... about ancient and modern learning." Sir William Temple had taken the side of the ancients against Charles Boyle, who had praised the ancient writer Phalaris, but Wotton and Bentley had taken Boyle's side. The controversy led to a battle between the books themselves, literally, in the King's library. The manuscript about the battle is incomplete, so we still do not know who won.

Then comes a preface from the author in which the nature of satire is discussed. Most people do not see themselves in the satire, seeing only others, and it is not a problem when someone sees himself and get offended, since in anger his counter-arguments are weak. Weak satires apply "wit without knowledge," while strong ones have depth.

The main tale begins with reflections about the causes of battles: mainly, pride and want. Like dogs, people fight over scarce resources but tend to be at peace during times of plenty.

The battle began, the story goes, when the Moderns, occupying the lower of the two tops of the hill Parnassus, grew jealous of the Ancients on the higher one. The Moderns offered to trade places or else to shovel down the higher hill, as a way of avoiding war, but the Ancients rejected the offer, surprised by the newcomers' insolence. The Moderns should raise themselves up instead. Yet the Moderns rejected that alternative and, being of greater numbers, always with new if weak recruits, chose war, with the pen as the chosen weapon. Despite defeats, both sides set up victory marks.

When the tales of victory are repeated often enough, the two sides become entrenched in "books of controversy" in the library. For example, Scotus made trouble for Plato by turning Aristotle against him, which led to a policy whereby upstarts would be chained up and kept away from the others. This policy worked until the Moderns became a force to be reckoned with, despite being "light-headed." Many of the Ancients had gotten out of place in the library as well, being stuck among the crowd of Moderns.

When the Moderns got ready for warfare, they got their best armor (ideas) from the Ancients. They claimed to be original, though, and since most of them had shoddy armor of their own making, Plato saw them and laughed in agreement that it was all their own.

There is a well-fed spider whose web-fortress is decorated "in the modern style" and who is best at science and mathematics. There is also a bee, who argues for the ancient values of "long search, much study, true judgment, and distinction of things" after getting caught briefly in the spider's web. The books are so transfixed by the discourse of the spider and the bee that they cease to quarrel.

Aesop takes the opportunity to escape to the side of the Ancients, remarking, characteristically, that the argument between bee and spider is a good allegory for that between Ancients and Moderns: the spider boasts "of his native stock and great genius," particularly in architecture and mathematics, while the bee and the Ancients are content "to pretend to nothing of our own beyond our wings and our voice" and "whatever [else] we have got has been by infinite labour and search, and ranging through every corner of nature."

This reflection inspires the books to prepare for battle, so they retreat to opposite sides of the library to choose their leaders and make their strategy. The moderns have lots of ugly weapons, some bulky fighters "without either arms, courage, or discipline," including Aquinas, and a crowd of "disorderly" and generally worthless writers. There are far more Moderns than Ancients, the Ancients being primarily Greeks (Homer, Plato, Aristotle, Hippocrates, Euclid, Herodotus) but also Romans such as Livy.

Fate alerts Jove about the impending battle, and (similarly to Homer's Iliad) there is a big meeting of the gods. Momus is on the side the Moderns; Pallas (Athena or her close relative) is on the side of the Ancients. Jove consults the book of Fate and learns what will happen regarding the battle, but he tells nobody.

Momus engages with the Goddess Criticism in order to gain victory. She sits upon a mountain next to Ignorance and Pride, her parents, along with others including Opinion, Noise, and the like. After hearing of the battle, she proceeds to dispense her critical bile where it can be made use of—especially in England. She arrives at the library to see her son Wotton. She disguises herself as Bentley (the book version) to speak with him. She encourages him and leaves helpers with him (named Dulness and Ill-manners).

The battle finally begins. Details of the battle, we learn, are missing in some of the alleged gaps in the text. Aristotle flings an arrow at Bacon, which misses and hits Descartes. Homer kills many. Virgil is a bit slow and his helmet is too big. Dryden appears, claiming descent from Virgil, and tricks Virgil into changing armor with him. (Virgil's was better.)

The Roman poet Lucan and the Modern epic poet Blackmore agree to exchange gifts and fight no more. The goddess Dulness gives the translator Thomas Creech a flying figure of the poet Horace to fight, but it goes badly for him—in the tradition of another poor translator, John Ogleby. The Greek poet Pindar slays many and finally faces the Modern named Abraham Cowley, to whom Pindar shows no mercy and cuts in two. Venus takes the better half of his body.

Summary and Analysis of "The Battle of the Books"

After another gap in the text comes "The Episode of Bentley and Wotton." The Moderns are almost ready to retreat when Bentley takes up their cause. He is contentious and "malignant," having a talent of lowbrow "railing," which is serviceable enough in politics, at least. He is rude to the Moderns and turns to his friend Wotton for help, The two of them march past the tomb of Aldrovandus, the Modern naturalist.

They find two Ancients asleep. Bentley goes forward while Wotton stands back. Bentley is about to kill an Ancient, when Affright (a child of one of the deities), sensing danger, stops him, with the two Ancients scaring him simply by moving in their sleep. He at least takes their armor.

Wotton, meanwhile, tries to drink at the fountain on Mt. Helicon (sacred to the Muses; the fountain is named Helicon), but Apollo prevents him from getting anything but mud. Wotton attempts to kill Sir William Temple (a Modern who seems to be on the Ancients' side) with divine help, but fails. Apollo is so furious at Wotton's attempt that Apollo orders Boyle to get revenge. Boyle catches up to the fleeing Wotton but, seeing Bentley with the armor, chases Bentley. The three of them fight. The divine Pallas helps Boyle. Bentley and Wotton are killed with a single stroke, and the two men die intertwined, almost indistinguishable from one another, like a pair of skewered woodcocks.

Analysis

Although the bookseller suggests that this story is not allegorical and not about real people, this story is very much an allegory. While the books may not be interchangeable with the authors, they at least represent the ideas contained within the books. It is not literally a battle of books. One can go far, however, simply by putting Swift's words in present-day English. Just restating the story in one's own words is in itself a demonstration of understanding, for doing so requires the reader to unravel the allegory.

The more you know of the works of each author mentioned, the better able you will be to see Swift's jokes and evaluate the claims behind them. For instance, is the great theologian Aquinas really "without either arms, courage, or discipline," or is this just an anti-religious bias? Is Thomas Creech really that bad a translator of Horace that the best way to (humorously) portray him is that he was pursuing a flying vision of Horace, created out of dullness, that was not even the real Horace? Homer is incredibly strong and able, implying that Swift considered him one of the best Ancients, defeating other writers with his works. When Aristotle flings an arrow at Bacon but hits Descartes, Swift is implying that Aristotle's work is superior to that of Descartes but perhaps not to Bacon's.

The allegory also works at a more general level. For example, the offer to level the Ancients' hill is a dig against the Moderns, who the author here casts as young upstarts who, at least in the eyes of the Ancients, should be grateful that they can labor under the protection of the Ancients' longstanding achievements. Instead, the Moderns seem to make a business out of rooting out problems in the Ancients' writings. The moderns are "light" intellectually but have large rears, yet they at least have numbers on their side.

The spider and bee also rather transparently represent, respectively, the Moderns and the Ancients. The spider is known for the scientific precision in his intricate web, yet the bee points out that he eats bugs instead of the nectar of better things, spewing out bile instead of honey, suggesting the relative advantages of each group.

It takes someone with knowledge of the Ancients to appreciate many of Swift's flourishes; the preference once again is for the Ancients. When it is said of the bee in the spider's web, "Thrice he endeavoured to force his passage, and thrice the centre shook," this is an allusion to dramatic passages of Homer, where for example Odysseus "thrice" tries to reach out for his mother in the Underworld. Likewise, the intervention of the gods in a battle is most likely an allusion to Homer's *Iliad*. The activity of the Goddess of Criticism with respect to her son Wotton, and the scenes of the battle in general, reflect similar scenes in the *Iliad*. The *Iliad*, for instance, contains an exchange of armor that is similar to the one here.

When the author "petition[s] for a hundred tongues, and mouths, and hands, and pens" in order to tell the tale of the battle itself, he is indeed drawing on epic writers, mainly Ancients, who called on the gods to help give them the language they need to capture the details. Aesop, master of fables (involving animals that signify humans), of course could be mistaken for a Modern when he takes the form of an ass.

Swift uses the deities to make further suggestions about the Ancients and Moderns. The Goddess of Criticism supports the Moderns along with Momus, god of satire, implying that criticism and mockery characterize the Moderns' writings. Swift of course is a modern satirist, so this does not simply mean that the modern satirists are all bad. Remember that there is "criticism" but also "true criticism," according to Swift's "Digression of the Modern Kind" in *A Tale of a Tub*. This Goddess, however, seems to represent much the worst kind, given her description as something like an ass full of spleen. The gods, for the most part, take the side of the Ancients and those few Moderns who are on the side of the Ancients.

In the final section, Swift parodies Bentley's and Wotton's close intellectual friendship and relatively weak abilities to fight the Ancients or even to drink at their fountain of wisdom. At the end, they are bound together just like in real life (in one book, both of their writings were bound together), basically indistinguishable. It is also comical that the great authors somehow need the help of these two men. It is fitting that when they die at the end, the battle rages on perfectly well without them. This is a lesson for other critics.

The gaps in the text permit Swift to turn easily from one topic to another. They also suggest the high degree to which the battle is unfinished, both overall and in the details of the conflicts between specific individuals. That the story ends without a conclusion might suggest the futility of the entire argument between Ancients and Moderns, since both sides have their virtues and each writer should be taken on his own merits. Given the intervention of the gods and the looming prophecy of Fate, there might not be much that men can do to affect the outcome.

Analysis

Summary and Analysis of "An Argument Against the Abolition of Christianity"

The full title of "An Argument Against the Abolishing of Christianity" is "An Argument to Prove That the Abolishing of Christianity in England May, As Things Now Stand, Be Attended With Some Inconveniences, and Perhaps Not Produce Those Many Good Effects Proposed Thereby." The author begins with the idea that while it is dangerous to take up a religious topic, especially when it is against the established leadership, he is resisting those who want to abolish Christianity. Not that long ago, the fashion was to be arguing the opposite, defending Christianity, as this author is doing now. Today, however, Christianity is out of fashion.

He assures his readers that he is not advocating for *true*, original Christianity, as this would be counter to all modern institutions. He says his purpose is to argue in favor of "nominal Christianity." Yet, in all fairness, he will examine both sides of the argument, the arguments both for and against abolishing the religion.

On the side of abolition is "liberty of conscience," which after all is a Protestant thing as well. Two people who genuinely had decided, after reflection, to be atheists were prosecuted for blasphemy, and a system of prosecution in the name of orthodoxy is likely to become very oppressive. Yet, if Christianity were abolished altogether, this kind of person who would enjoy the ornery nature of being an atheist would, instead, rail against the nobility and the government.

Likewise, it has been said that Freethinkers are unfairly forced to believe difficult things that were not ingrained from youth, even though it is unclear how much education in Christianity the people really have after all. People seem to do quite well in their professions without much learning, so it is not quite right to suggest that most people live their lives on the basis of Christian doctrine. In response, however, Christianity provides at least a small number of people with the intellectual resources that the civilization will need to depend on, even if their number is few.

The next argument for abolition is that people would be allowed to work on Sundays, which would have economic benefits, and the churches could be used for other purposes. Yet, a lot of people already do not go to church, which was the presumed purpose of the day of rest. The coffee-houses stay open on Sundays, for instance, and many people go to them. Busy people just do their work at home. Besides, churches give everyone a chance to meet and make business deals, to dress up for one another, or at least to sleep.

The narrator says that the best advantage of abolishing Christianity, people say, if it would really happen, would be the end of party divisions, both religious and political. This would be wonderful. This would be unlikely, however, because people would not suddenly become rational, moral beings. People are prone to form factions regardless of religion. Just getting religious words about the vices out of the language would not make the underlying human vices disappear. Abolishing Christianity might ultimately unify the Protestant sects, but new divisions will spring up.

The narrator next addresses the hypocrisy of pursuing one kind of life six days of the week, then repenting on the seventh. Yet, the enjoyment of sinning is precisely why men sometimes engage in certain activities--because they are forbidden. Why would a Freethinker want to abolish Christianity and forgo the pleasure? Christianity gives people something to do and gives them a club, and there are always people who enjoy either being insiders or being outsiders.

Next, people have suggested that abolishing Christianity would eradicate prejudices of education, but these are either so deeply entrenched that they are likely to exist even after abolition--or, as for most people, words like "justice" are so far from actual beliefs as to be irrelevant to nominal Christianity. The English are just as good at being unbelievers as the best Freethinkers! Even so, there seems to be some use in Christianity for the true Christians among the vulgar poor, who can be better kept under control by religion.

The narrator now examines arguments in favor of keeping Christianity legal, focusing on the problems that would be incurred by its abolition. First, without Christianity, men of wit would have nothing to mock and would mock each other instead. There are many complaints that wit is on the decline, yet Christianity offers the best material.

Next, abolishing the existing form of Christianity from the state would open the door for the contemporary church to be replaced with an even less traditional version, under the influence of deists and others, or for Catholicism to make its return. Those who are concerned about the survival of the church after abolition should consider that it might be fundamentally changed. Besides, the people will find some new superstition in any case.

The narrator concludes by offering that it might make more sense to ban all religion instead of just Christianity. The ultimate problem is the basic belief in God and Providence, which prevents people from acting freely. At least, that is what the Freethinkers believe, being generally opposed to religion in part because they like to be ornery and do what they please. Finally, if people are not persuaded, at least they should wait to abolish Christianity until a time of international peace, because it could put the British Empire in a very vulnerable position, since there are no atheist nations to be allied with. Besides, if the Act passes, stocks will go down much more than has been expended recently to preserve the religion, and there is no good reason to take the financial loss just to get rid of the religion.

Analysis

The narrator appears to take care at the beginning to say that he does not intend to advocate for original Christianity because it would be too disruptive to contemporary society. This is a biting start, taking the side of radical Protestants in theory, those who wanted to clear away all of the seemingly non-Christian traditions that had gotten in the way of the original doctrine. Yet, in practice, this would be too disruptive for the same reason that the radical reformer ruins his coat in *Tale of a Tub*; ripping out all the extraneous matter will ruin what is good in the tradition as well. Besides, one of the main arguments is that the contemporary English are so irreligious already that the fabric of the religion has already been ripped apart or ignored as people go about their business uneducated and unconcerned about their hypocrisy.

The voice speaking in this piece is that of a rich fop. We might first infer this from the narrator's warning against atheists, who would turn against the nobility if they had too much chance. Swift returns to his common project of mocking the upper classes with this tone. The narrator also uses the phrase "gentlemen of wit and pleasure" (a phrase used by the rich to describe themselves). Also, with the argument that going to church provides the opportunity of showing off one's "advantage of dress," the narrator appears to be one of the elite who has something to show off--and therefore is all the more worthy of ridicule. At the same time, however, the narrator appears to understand quite well that he is calling out his fellow citizens on their religious hypocrisy. And at other points, he seems to be a fellow traveler with atheist freethinkers, showing them how on their own grounds they should ensure that Christianity is not entirely abolished.

The immediate purpose of this piece is not to poke fun at the upper class, at any rate, but to advocate against the repeal of the Test Act of 1671, which required officials to take communion with the Church of England before assuming public positions. The "abolishing of Christianity" in this piece is akin to the repeal of the Test Act. Swift was in favor of keeping the act in place, which is why he chose to align his opponents with the "sinful" position of the abolition of Christianity. It is of note that the main conflict in religious life was not between Christians and atheists, but between Catholics and Protestants; the main group that would be helped by repealing the Test Act would be Catholics, who did not consider themselves to be in communion with Protestants.

Even so, Christianity comes in for quite a lot of ribbing, since the essay, standing on its own terms, is about Christianity overall and not the very specific question of the Test Act. The ultimate problem that the narrator identifies, at least from the Freethinking perspective of freedom of conscience and action, where justice depends on reason instead of faith, is the basic belief in God and Providence. This is an early version of an argument made later by, for example, Nietzsche, in determining that religion interferes with people's moral choices rather than helping them along.

In the case of "A Modest Proposal," the suggestion being advocated would never be adopted. In the case of "An Argument Against the Abolition of Christianity," the suggestion of abolishing the religion would never be adopted, either. Swift is doing something different here, though, because here he is not proposing something but is challenging a proposal. He is arguing about the disadvantages of something that was never going to happen anyway (apart from the specific question of the Test Act). Here he is taking the risky position of making a position that he agrees with look ridiculous, even while the position he supposedly disagrees with looks ridiculous, too.

Swift here has provided a very strange set of arguments in that he rarely takes the point of view of a contemporary Christian. The reaction of the Christian reader of his time was likely that there are far better reasons for maintaining the religion that Swift is not mentioning, thus bringing the reader over to his view by letting the reader supply the better arguments. Yet, what does Swift believe? Is he so opposed to Catholics because he prefers Protestants, or is he enough of a dissenter to be opposed to them both, with Protestants being more latitudinarian and more free, the lesser of two evils? Would he be content with original rather than nominal Christianity? The satire here is unclear, perhaps intentionally so.

Summary and Analysis of "A Modest Proposal"

"A Modest Proposal" begins with an account of the impoverished state of many in Ireland. The writer expresses sympathy and the need for a solution. This proposal hopefully will decrease the number of abortions performed by poor mothers. The writer calculates the number of infants born in Ireland and asks what should be done with them. He points out that they are unfit for any employment, being even too young to steal. Neither will merchants buy or sell children. Therefore, it seems like a good idea that the people of Ireland simply eat the infants when they reach the age of one year.

The writer treats the weight of an infant, what kind of dish it will make, and how many people it will serve. He surmises the times of year when the infants will be most plentiful, based on the purported sexual patterns of the Irish. There might also be uses for the discarded skin of the infants, such as for ladies' gloves.

A friend of the narrator's, "a very worthy person," has already heard the proposal and suggested that children of fourteen, too, be a potential food. The writer has dismissed this idea, though, because the flesh of fourteen-year-old boys is too lean, and fourteen-year-old girls might soon become breeders of infants themselves. He defends his friend, nevertheless, by saying that the friend learned of this practice in Asia among certain savage peoples. This digression continues with the observation that he is unconcerned about those adults who are ill, disabled, or starving, because there is nothing he can do for them.

He returns to the chief proposal and lists six reasons why it should be adopted. First, it will decrease the number of dangerous Catholics. Second, it will give the poor some property. Third, it will increase the nation's overall wealth, since people will not have to pay for the upkeep of the children. Fourth, the mothers will be free of the burden of bringing up children. Fifth, the new food will be welcomed in taverns and culinary circles. Sixth, it will enhance the institution of marriage as women take better care of their infants so that they may be sold, and men will take better care of their wives so that their wives can make more babies to sell.

Swift then raises a potential objection to his proposal: that it will deplete Ireland's population. Swift responds by saying that this is the point. He says that this proposal will in no way encumber England, as the infants will not be able to be exported, as their flesh is not easily preserved for later consumption. He is not willing to entertain any other arguments for solving the problem, like virtue and thrift.

Swift concludes by saying first that he would welcome any other suggestions anyone may have on this question, then assuring the reader that he has no personal economic stake in this idea because he has no children and therefore could not profit by selling them to be eaten.

Analysis

If you do not realize that this proposal is satirical, you have no sense of humor or irony. It is impossible to imagine a serious proposal for eating children. Yet, it is not enough simply to indulge one's outrage over the argument or to smile at the jokes. Is Swift just having fun, or does he have something serious to say?

Stereotypes against Irish Catholics make it easier for Swift to use them as the subject of his satire. The stereotypes are present in both the reasons for the proposal and the language used. The narrator's argument that something must be done with infants because they are too young to steal implies that this is a common employment of Irish Catholics, even while it is humorous apart from the stereotype. The overall idea of overpopulation comes from the stereotype that Catholics tend to have a lot of children. The first reason Swift's narrator gives for adopting his proposal—that it will lessen the number of Catholics—is perhaps the best example of satire of religious prejudice in the piece. Furthermore, he uses the word "papists" in the offensive sense of anti-Catholic rejection of the Pope. In Protestant England, many people might share the stereotypes but would never go so far as the speaker suggests about eating children.

The theme of prejudice against the lower classes is revealed in suggestions such as the idea that the carcasses of the poor children could be used for clothing, women's gloves. Swift suggests, with this extreme example, as well as his declaration that the landlords have already "devoured" the poor infants' parents, that the rich live at the expense of the poor. By referring next to another figure, "a very worthy person" (who is meant to represent a member of the upper, learned classes), Swift furthers his satire of the upper classes by implying that there are people so disconnected from the lower classes that they might agree with this outlandish proposal.

Swift's aim, however, was not merely to expose England's biased view of Ireland or to illuminate general English arrogance towards other peoples, although the latter aim is achieved. The narrator's statement that an "American" told him that children are "delicious" parodies the idea that the Americans, like the Irish, were considered to be a barbaric people in need of instruction from the English. So, too, does the reference to the island of Formosa evoke a kind of English cultural arrogance. All people who could be classified as "other" are potentially dangerous to the English, needing to be tamed.

"A Modest Proposal" is also literary commentary. Swift intended to parody similar pamphlets that were being circulated at the time. His diction throughout the piece, including the word *modest* in the title, highlights this effect. Of course, one's proposals are modest and offered "humbly." With word choice like this, Swift is mocking the false modesty in the tone of many of the pamphlets of his contemporaries; their style may have professed deference, but their proposals displayed audacity.

Swift finally gets down to some real arguments when the narrator lists all the arguments that he will not give any time to. If eating the children were off the table, the people would have to turn to realistic arguments like these, such as the encouragement of virtue and thrift.

"A Modest Proposal" is accurately called one of the most effective satires in the English language. There are a few key moments of satirical success that should be mentioned. Swift's decision to put off the actual suggestion of eating babies until several paragraphs into the piece makes his idea all the more arresting when it does come. Also, naming population decrease as the one potential objection to his proposal, Swift heightens the irony of an already ironic piece. The reader is expecting this objection to be that it is morally wrong to kill babies, but Swift subverts our expectations once again, suggesting that there are people so cold to reality that they could be swayed by merely practical economic arguments and cannot even see the outrage of cannibalism.

Finally, when the writer reassures the reader that he has nothing to gain economically from his proposal, for he has no children, Swift is playing on the common protestation of writers that their political and social proposals are made altruistically for the good of society and should therefore be believed to be all the more sincere. If the writer did have children and lived in Ireland, it would be consistent to eat them or sell them.

Swift, by 1729, was quite late in his career, being already over 60 years old. If his more careful, complex, difficult satires had not been sufficiently understood and appreciated, it was time to bang the people over the head with a satire that they could recognize and which would renew interest in his other works. Although *Gulliver's Travels* was fresh in people's minds, it was already 25 years after *A Tale of a Tub*. Anyone who becomes intrigued by Jonathan Swift after reading "A Modest Proposal" should go on to the works that are worthy of a more sophisticated critic.

Summary and Analysis of "A True and Faithful Narrative"

"A True and Faithful Narrative" begins with a lecture given by Mr. Whiston at the Royal Exchange. The narrator lists the men who were present at the lecture. Mr. Whiston declares that he cannot make his prepared lecture, and pauses for a long time, apparently in mental effort or prayer. He predicts that next Friday, the world will end because a comet will strike. The comet will appear in the sky at five minutes after five.

Within a couple of hours, everyone in the city is aware of the prediction. The narrator struggles with the negligence of his religious duty. He speaks with his Quaker friend, who doubts the prediction. The comet appears in the sky on Wednesday morning, however, just as Mr. Whiston predicted.

Clergymen assemble to offer prayers. The narrator goes to church with his wife for the first time in many weeks, and they encounter a large crowd. Powerful, rich men fear the judgment and review their lives with worry. The young ladies get ready to appear naked at judgment by bathing themselves. The lawyers likewise worry about their fate, and judges are relieved that they are no longer attorneys. The soldiers in the army are quite content. The physicians appear to be unmoved but display signs of religious conviction. Among the clergy, the higher his position is, the greater is his fear.

A few people express joy, including criminals who were to be executed. A man who has been a churchgoer all his life and is now deadly ill, likewise is pleased with the news.

The day before the comet has been predicted to strike, business slows down in the city. There are, however, rushes on the banks, and there are several thousand marriages between men and their mistresses.

The wealthy begin to give their money away to the beggars. A few very rich and powerful members of town give a large donation to the church. Many ladies make confessions to their husbands that one or more of their children are bastards.

As the day approaches, everyone is in church, although none of the religious denominations join and pray together, because they believe that the others are to be damned, and they alone will be saved.

By the end of the day on Friday, the comet has not stuck. The population begins to mock the prophecy. They disown the idea that they displayed any signs of religion. They spend the next day in their usual sinful activities.

Analysis

The first aspect of satire here comes in the person of Mr. Whiston and the prediction itself. Swift is making fun of these public lectures in which people make grand declarations that have little to do with reality. Swift suggests that sometimes these predictions may have the *appearance* of truth but nothing else; the prophecy is false.

The prophecy was not completely false; depending on which comet it was, a good scientist in theory could have predicted its appearance. Just like those who predict eclipses and thereby amaze and control a superstitious population, Whiston has, perhaps by chance, stunned the population into moral compliance with religion.

Swift also satirizes specific aspects of society within this piece. His poor opinion of lawyers is expressed in his decision to make the lawyers incredibly nervous as the day of judgment approaches. His argument that the upper classes do not lead a Christian life is expressed in the elaborate charitable gifts made several prominent men and women, who at the least think they can earn a spiritual benefit through their last-minute donation. The ideal person is the longtime churchgoer who is consistent about his principles and practices regardless of the date of the end of the world, a person represented by the churchgoing sick man who is joyful about the end of the world.

Ultimately, Swift is satirizing a society's religious hypocrisy in general, implying that people are naturally sinful and prone to slip in their convictions. Swift suggests that religion is entirely an expedient for most people, serving their immediate needs. He pokes fun at the displays of religious excess in the story, which he does not portray as sincere. The narrator himself is a sinful man who has not been to church in weeks and who does not intend to go to church until he believes he is about to die. Similarly, the entire population of the town is sinful prior to the prediction, quickly returning to their sinful behavior when the prediction proves to be false.

Religious excess and hypocrisy are common themes in Swift's satires. He addresses these topics with force in "A True and Faithful Narrative" in a way that many readers would understand. Instead of getting the point across by argument or hiding it in allegory, Swift gives the people a story with a fairly plain meaning.

Summary and Analysis of "A Meditation upon a Broomstick"

"A Meditation upon a Broomstick" begins with the narrator's lament that he used to know "this single stick" when it was a part of a beautiful tree, and now it is used to make things clean by getting itself dirty. The fate of "this single stick" is ultimately the fire.

The narrator reveals that his subject is a broomstick. He declares that a broomstick is like a man. He is born upright, with all his hair, but is turned upside down, then relegated to a "withered trunk" as he ages. Man lives according to the whim of maids, much like the broomstick. Man reveals abuses, sweeps up dirt, and participates in the very pollution he pretends to want to eradicate. Man's fate, like that of the stick, is either to be kicked out of doors or to be used for criticism by others.

Analysis

The main purpose of "A Meditation Upon a Broomstick," a short piece in just two paragraphs, is literary parody. Swift is mocking the writing style of Robert Boyle, whom he considered to be a "very silly writer." The specific book that Swift is parodying is *Occasional Reflections Upon Several Subjects*, which Swift considered a silly title (almost as silly as "A Meditation Upon a Broomstick"). Swift's attempts to poke fun at Boyle's language are apparent in his woeful, lamenting tone, in such lines as, "When I beheld this I sighed, and said within myself, Surely mortal man is a Broomstick!" (p. 231).

Swift also presents a piece that is humorous in itself. It turns out that man is very like a broomstick, often being upside-down and irrational, sweeping up and raking up dirt as people criticize one another, and becoming soiled in the process.

Suggested Essay Questions

1. Give examples of satire in "A Modest Proposal" and describe why they are satirical.

   Answer: The entirety of "A Modest Proposal" is satirical because it makes fun of other grand ideas that people have proposed to solve big problems in society. The proposal itself—that the Irish should eat their babies—is satirical, too, because it makes fun of people who propose absurd things thinking that they are practical. Swift's reference to boys and girls as not a "saleable commodity" is a good particular example because it suggests the cold thinking of people who argue for turning everything into questions of economics. A similar moment comes when Swift says that "those who are thrifty" may use the carcass of the infant for ladies' gloves or gentlemen's boots; this takes children as animals where the whole animal is used for different purposes. The narrator's friend, the "very worthy person," proposes that children of fourteen should be consumed as well, and the honest assessment of this idea is satirical along the same lines; the taste is what matters and, besides, it would limit the number of breeders (which is itself a strange argument if overpopulation or too many Irishmen were the problem). Swift's final declaration that he has nothing to gain economically from his proposal satirizes the usual protestations of people who are claiming to be altruistic in their proposals.

2. Discuss the theme of religious prejudice in Swift's satires.

   Answer: "A Modest Proposal" takes on the theme of religious prejudice with the narrator's assurance that his proposal that Ireland eat its young will decrease the number of "papists" (Roman Catholics). Assuming the narrative voice of a bigoted English Protestant, Swift says that the Irish Catholics are England's "dangerous enemies." Swift exposes the stereotype (taken here as a negative) that Catholics have many children by having his narrator call them the "chief breeders of the nation." In "An Argument Abolishing Christianity," too, Swift assumes the voice of someone with religious prejudices in order to expose those prejudices. The narrator says that the abolition of Christianity could invite "papists" (again, Catholics) to invade England or would give Freethinkers a lot less enjoyment in sinning or making fun of Christians. "A True and Faithful Narrative" points out Swift's own prejudice, shared by many (perhaps because it is basic to human nature), that religious people tend to be hypocritical and unwilling to live up to their own ideals.

3. Why did Swift publish "A Modest Proposal" anonymously? How does this contribute to the effectiveness of his piece?

   Answer: If Swift had not published his piece anonymously, readers may have been less likely to consider it serious. If readers knew from the beginning that "A Modest Proposal" was written by an accomplished satirist, they would be looking for the joke from the beginning and might not be taken in at all. The proposed solution for the poverty in Ireland might have been believed for just long enough to make readers appreciate the deeper level of satire against cold and calculating arguments that miss the elements of basic humanity. Assuming the guise of a fake, anonymous narrator allowed him to better parody the prejudices that someone like his narrator might have.

4. What attitude does "A Modest Proposal" take to the trend of answering social questions with mathematics?

Answer: "A Modest Proposal" mocks the idea that society's ills can be cured by simple calculations. The piece is full of numbers: the number of people in the entire country, the number of couples, the number of poor couples, the number of children born into poor families, and many more. Swift conducts mathematics with these numbers in his proposal, subtracting, for example, the number of miscarriages or deaths by famine or disease from the total number of children born per year. By turning a tragic thing like the death of children into a math problem, Swift is mocking the tendency in the nineteenth century to view social questions dispassionately in terms of calculations, according to the new advances in science, math, and economics, instead of considering the human element.

5. Discuss the theme of economic inequality in "A Modest Proposal."

Answer: Economic inequality was a chief concern of Swift's, and he expressed this concern satirically in "A Modest Proposal." The title itself hints at economic inequality—his proposal applies to "the poor people of Ireland." The children that will be eaten, under this proposal, are poor children. Specifically, the poor children will be bought and eaten by the rich. This is only right, says the narrator, because the rich have already consumed their parents economically. Swift is making the point that economic exploitation is like actual consumption; the rich feed off the poor.

6. Why might Jonathan Swift have chosen to write so much satire? What is he able to do with a satirical piece that he is unable to do with a serious piece?

Answer: If Jonathan Swift had written serious pieces simply espousing his true beliefs—for instance, that the state of the poor in Ireland was deplorable, that something must be done to help them—he would have likely gotten little response, as there were many such pamphlets circulating at the time. It was hard enough to write a lasting piece in any genre, and at least people like to criticize and they like to laugh. A satirical parody (a shocking one in particular) was likely to get the public's attention in ways that a seriously written piece could not achieve. "A Modest Proposal" surprised people and got them thinking about the condition of the poor in Ireland and what should seriously be done about it. And when very sensitive subjects are involved, such as criticizing the nation's prevailing religion, it is much safer to be hard to read and to be seemingly joking rather than to directly challenge authority.

7. Is Swift's "main objection" to his idea in "A Modest Proposal" a sincere objection? How does this contribute to the effectiveness of the piece?

Answer: If any reader still thinks that this is a serious piece by this point, the "main objection" ought to persuade them that it is not. The writer says that the main objection to the killing and eating of Irish young is that it will decrease the population. A truly serious objection from a normal human being would be that it is morally wrong to consume human flesh on such a large scale. Furthermore, it is a straw-man objection, since the author reminds the reader that reducing the population is the overall goal anyway. Taking up the real objections would distract the reader by introducing a level of seriousness that the reader already knows how to reply. Besides, Swift introduces indirectly a good objection: that there are better ways to fix the problem, and the narrator even lists a bunch of ideas while saying that he is not interested to consider them. The effectiveness of the piece comes in large measure because the reader becomes engaged in thinking about the real problem and real solutions.

8. What is going on in the battle of the Ancients and the Moderns in "The Battle of the Books?" Are they truly two separate sides?

Answer: Although the Ancients and the Moderns appear to be two distinct sides in "The Battle of the Books," there is evidence in the text of their similarity. They fight in the same world over the same territory, and the librarian, for better or for worse, has mixed the Ancients and Moderns together in the library, presumably on the basis of subject matter. The most worthy Moderns use the best of what can be found in the Ancients. The spider and the bee, the allegorical representations of the two sides, are themselves embroiled; the bee gets caught in the spider's web. Their sources of disagreement, too, do not seem irreconcilable. The quarrel has a lot to do with those Moderns who turn up their noses at the Ancients and arrogantly go on their own way, and with the great swarm of third-rate Moderns who try to make a name for themselves by tearing down the great works and great ideas of the Ancients, or who like to quarrel with one another about the actual value of the Ancients. Certain characters in "The Battle of the Books" are more successful in battle than others based on how Swift judges their literary quality; despite Swift's usual preference for the best of the Ancients, sometimes a great Modern overcomes a weak Ancient.

9. Give examples of Jonathan Swift's literary parody.

Answer: "A Modest Proposal" is a parody of pamphlets distributed at the time that professed to have the single cure for all social problems. Swift thought this "can-do" attitude with its prescriptive writing style was naïve. The introductory material and digressions in *A Tale of a Tub* are themselves parodies of a variety of types of writing: medical texts, religious texts, and political texts, as well as the kinds of things written in introductions and by booksellers. "Meditation Upon a Broomstick" is a parody of the writing style of Swift's contemporary Robert Boyle. "The Battle of the Books" parodies many scenes in Homer's war epic, the *Iliad*. His satires thus not only parody ideas and personalities but also certain ways of expressing those ideas.

10. Write an essay in Swift's style.

Answer: Think of a political or social issue, preferably something relevant to your own place and time. If you choose school uniforms, for example, the next step is to come up with your idea of the problem that is supposedly being solved. Then, decide where you stand on the issue: do school uniforms solve the problem or not? Next, think of a way of expressing this solution that would be extreme (like eating babies in "A Modest Proposal"). For example, if the idea of uniforms is uniformity and you do not think this is a good enough reason for school uniforms, then you could make fun of it by arguing that the students should go to school naked. Your essay will then be in the voice of someone who believes the opposite, arguing for attending school naked for the sake of uniformity (just like Swift's narrator argued that Ireland should eat its young, but Swift didn't actually believe this, and like Swift made those in favor of repealing the Test Act seem to be anti-Christianity in "An Argument Against Abolishing Christianity"). Now, choose a method of literary parody. Maybe you will pretend that this is an opinion piece in the school newspaper. This helps establish your audience and the kind of writing you will make fun of. Now comes the hardest part of all: telling all the jokes in the way that Swift does. As you think of the reasons that your extreme solution might be purportedly a good idea, imagine what different people might be thinking—parents, teachers, politicians, prudes, nudists. These reasons can be as silly as you want to make them, and if you have some extra joke to make about these kinds of people, fold them into the arguments. You could say, for example, that going to school naked would mean that parents wouldn't have to pay for their students' clothes, which is an expensive thing because students are always trying to get their parents to pay for the latest faddish designers. Or you could say that going to school naked would keep students from developing tan lines, or reduce the need for "sexting" because everyone would already know what each other looks like naked. The more different levels of satire you can get to work at the same time, the more it will be in the style of Swift.

Swift's "Muses"

Swift, as a satirical writer, often gained inspiration from men and ideas that he considered to be ridiculous. He was motivated to write in parody of them. Others he admired greatly. A few of his contemporaries, however, were more "muse-like" than others in terms of their influence on Swift. Here are a few of these men.

Lord John Somers (1651-1716)

Somers appears in *A Tale of a Tub*. Swift hailed Somers as "one of the greatest men of his age and nation." Somers was a Whig politician who was crucial in the Revolution Settlement and the creation of the Bill of Rights in England. He rose to the position of Lord High Chancellor under William III. He published several treatises about politics with which Swift undoubtedly was familiar. While Swift was an admirer of his, Somers' own record was mixed. He advocated for greater rights, but, ultimately, these rights were only enjoyed by an elite. In *Tale of a Tub*, Swift parodies the figure of the unliterary bookseller by having the bookseller write a dedication to Somers (a truly powerful and influential figure), but Somers is not spared either in Swift's parody; the bookseller says that he is writing to Somers because the author says the book is about vanity, and Somers is a vain man.

Robert Boyle (1627-1691)

Boyle may be best known for Boyle's Law, which states that the pressure and volume of a gas are inversely proportional at constant temperature. Boyle was a writer who Swift parodied in "A Meditation Upon a Broomstick." Like Swift, Boyle was a Renaissance man, writing on a variety of topics including science, politics, and theology. Swift called Boyle "a very silly writer." The book that Swift was parodying specifically was *Occasional Reflections Upon Several Subjects*, which Butler also parodied with his book *An Occasional Reflection on Dr. Charlton's Feeling a Dog's Pulse at Gresham College. Occasional Reflections* is far from being Boyle's most well-known work, or most influential; if it hadn't been for the parodies, it may have been forgotten. The book was ripe for parody, however, as it was a bizarre grouping of unrelated thoughts and musings presented in a deadly serious manner. Note that Robert Boyle is not the same person as the hero at the end of "The Battle of the Books"—that person is Charles Boyle, a translator of the ancient writer Phalaris (a tyrant known for allegedly having eaten human babies).

Sir William Petty (1623-1687)

Petty was most influential on Swift's "A Modest Proposal." Petty was an economist and scientist known for his theories of "political arithmetic." He believed that all one needed to solve political or social questions was to ask and solve the right math questions. He was one of the early proponents of laissez-faire economic policy. Swift considered Petty, and those like him, to be taking a hard-hearted approach to social questions. Swift's many numbers and cold economic calculations in "A Modest Proposal" come in large part from Petty's "political arithmetic."

Alexander Pope (1688-1744)

Pope was one of Swift's friends and a fellow satirist. Pope was best known for his heroic couplet style of poetry. Pope and Swift came from similarly disadvantaged positions from an English Protestant perspective: Pope was Catholic; Swift was Irish. They both exposed social prejudices in their writing. Specifically, Pope's masterful "The Rape of the Lock," an epic poem about a minor event (the unwanted cutting off of a lock of a girl's hair), was influential on Swift's commentary on economic inequality in both *Gulliver's Travels* and "A Modest Proposal." Swift was likely also thinking of Pope when writing "The Battle of the Books," because Pope was a champion of the Ancients. The two men corresponded often by letter, which also suggests the degree to which Pope was important in Swift's life. Although Pope's medium was poetry and Swift's was prose, the two were both satirists, and Pope undoubtedly influenced Swift's projects.

Author of ClassicNote and Sources

Cora Frazier, author of ClassicNote. Completed on March 23, 2010, copyright held by GradeSaver.

Updated and revised Adam Kissel May 30, 2010. Copyright held by GradeSaver.

Swift, Jonathan. A Modest Proposal and Other Satires. Hungary: Konemann, 1997.

Swift, Jonathan, ed. Carole Fabricant. A Modest Proposal and Other Writings. London: Penguin Books, 2009.

Sachse, William Lewis. Lord Somers: A Political Portrait. Madison: The University of Madison Press, 1975.

Conner, Tamsen (Brown University). "Satire and Significance in Jonathan Swift's 'A Modest Proposal'." 2005-02-09. 2010-03-03. <http://www.victorianweb.org/previctorian/swift/conner2.html>.

Smith, Nicole. "Social Critique, Irony, and Satire in 'A Modest Proposal' and Candide." Article Myriad. 2010-03-02. <http://www.articlemyriad.com/175.htm>.

Bragg, Melvyn, and guests. "Swift's 'A Modest Proposal'." BBC Radio. 2009-07-29. 2010-03-06. <http://www.bbc.co.uk/programmes/b00h3650>.

"Robert Boyle: Irish Chemist (1627-91)." 1902 Encyclopedia. 2010-03-25. <http://www.1902encyclopedia.com/B/BOY/robert-boyle.html>.

Power, Max. "Alexander Pope and Jonathan Swift: Differing Philosophies with Identical Conclusions." Associated Content. 2007-01-22. 2010-03-24. <http://www.associatedcontent.com/article/122465/jonathan_swift_and_alexander_pope_diffe

Essay: A Modest Proposal

by Anonymous
February 06, 2003

In his essay, A Modest Proposal, Jonathan Swift uses the literary devices of organization, point of view, diction and imagery to maneuver the reader into identifying the need for humans to let both logic and emotion govern decisions.

Jonathan Swift, in order to prepare his audience for his radical proposal to provide for the large starving Irish population, first identifies the problem and provides hard facts before stating his actual scheme, so that the reader may see the logic in his otherwise horrifying plan of eating Irish infants. In the first five paragraphs, Swift addresses the problem of Ireland's huge starving population as an unfortunate predicament, but not one of his own concerns. His explanation appeals to those indifferent about the plight of the Irish beggars, such as the English, informing them of a regrettable fact. However, in the sixth paragraph, in his last attempt to gain the audience's support, he resorts to dry facts, hoping that the readers will abandon emotional ties and regard this problem and its solution with only logic and reason. Swift's organization of the essay, particularly his deliberate delay in stating the thesis, gives him a certain power, by which he shares with the audience ideas that, unprepared for, they would have immediately rejected.

In narrating his essay, Swift chooses to write as a naÃ¯ve narrator who actually takes the side of the people he is trying to chastise. By writing from the point of view of a person not at all sympathetic of the Irish condition then over exaggerating as to the inconvenience the beggars pose on the sophisticated elite and proposing such an absurd and grotesque solution, Swift illustrates the actual preposterousness of Irish oppression, and his true feelings towards the English exploitation of the Irish. Since, in the narrator's opinion, the beggars contribute to the "deplorable state of the kingdom", a concern of only the wealthy, Swift almost comically shows how inconsiderate and self-absorbed the wealthy are to think that the poor, living in abject poverty, are merely an unsightly nuisance. Swift counts on his audience seeing through the shallow narrator and come to the conclusion that you must rely on emotion as well as logic when considering how to provide for the Irish. Emotional ties are dealt with ironically throughout the piece, noticeable first in Swift's comment about the "horrid practice" of abortions and killing illegitimate children, which seems not as immoral considering his plan of killing and eating children a year old, then again when he says in all sincerity that he could not experience the least personal gain, since his youngest child was too old to be eaten. By writing from the point of view opposite to his own, Swift easily has his narrator highlight the mistakes and faults of the English, and can sway the reader's opinions to agree with his own.

Swift's choice of diction in A Modest Proposal enables him to control the reader's opinion of the society and its treatment of the Irish. The powerful words he uses, such as describing the Irish as animals, helps the narrator justify butchering and eating children. However, when the different methods of cooking children are discussed, he relies on the compassion and ethics his audience retains to turn the readers against the narrator. Breeding humans like livestock is unthinkable; it disregards emotional ties and morals, which is what sets humans above animals. The vivid descriptions tie the "proposal" to cannibalism, a crime that would bring humans down, from the role as the superior race, to the level of hyenas and other uncivilized animals. Through his word choice, Jonathan Swift successfully illustrates the failure of the English intervention and feudal governing techniques thus far.

Essay: "A Modest Proposal" Tone Essay

by Anonymous
March 30, 2007

A Modest Proposal Tone Essay

The extensive use of satire by Jonathan Swift in his work A Modest Proposal presents his idea on how to terminate a major problem in Ireland: poverty. The tone of the passage varies dramatically throughout its development; it changes from very serious to sarcastic.

Swift begins by portraying the poor people and their children and the consequences of it: "... as they grow up, either turn thieves for want of work, or leave their dear native country, to fight for the Pretender in Spain..." Through this quote Swift is contemplating on the problem that alludes to having poor children and the consequences of this on the Irish society. Through the excerpt, it is seen how Swift begins by persuading the intended audience that there should be a solution created in order to stop the problem caused by the excess of poor people. Having contemplated on the topic, he then discusses in a serious tone the fact that action must be taken in order to stop the problem from further expansion. "A statue should be set up for a preserver of nation". This quote refers to how Swift is serious about the issue and is trying to find a solution to it.

Swift contemplates on the issue and begins to calculate statistically the number of children who are born; "the number of souls in this kingdom being usually reckoned one million and a half..." This quote shows how his tone is beginning to have a shift through desperateness by describing how they are worthless to society and there must be a solution: "the question therefore is how this number shall be reared..." Through this quote Swift is developing on the seriousness of the issue that is being faced and his desire to find a solution. In his desire to come up with a solution, Swift proposes a solution: "I humbly propose my own thoughts" hoping not to be "liable to the least objection" Swift begins in his Modest Proposal by presenting how "a young healthy child well nursed, is at a year old, a most delicious nourishing and wholesome food" The tone then has a shift has from serious tone to sarcastic. Swift's ideas range from eating babies to making clothes out of their skin: "...gloves for ladies and summer boots for fine gentlemen..."

Swift's work then becomes inhumane through the insipid ideas in coming up with a solution. The other kingdom which believes on Swifts concept believe how children will satisfy the "want of venison". Through the descriptions given by Jonathan Swift, the tone becomes disgusting in its own way, how it talks about children being prepared to serve as food and clothing, at the same time as the problem is being eradicated.

Jonathan Swift idealistic proposals to persuade the intended audience are expressed through the use of descriptive examples that bring the reader to the tone of the passage. Making inhuman proposals increases the importance of the problem, only to allow the reader to understand that in reality there is no useful solution to the problem provided in the essay. Swift contemplates on how his proposals have become insipid, on a exasperation to finding a solution to ending poverty.

Mock "Modest Proposal":

To whom it may concern (any form of government),

I compose this modest proposal with the intention of offering an expedient to lessen the ineffectiveness of your government. Unlike your ideals, those of an authentic communism are of real concern. This government is to the advantage of all, no just merchants and those with property. But what about our children? They deserve to live in a society of common advantage of all members that can be achieved with an authentic communism, yet unknown to the world. The communist governments that have existed and the prudent intervention of the United States to eradicate what is not convenient to capitalism have given a misconception to the world about this economic system. But otherwise, how would we be able to exploit the citizens of third-world countries to make our goods at incredibly low costs when communism does not permit this? Thinking about it, maybe we should just stick to your worthy government after all. The valuable discount that we get justifies our abusiveness towards those countries that we find in the tags of our clothes. This allows us to be thrifty shoppers and overflow our closets with plentiful garments, and our living rooms with abundant technology. Pardon me I ever mentioned the wrongs in the existing government; let me pretend our avarice does harm to nobody.

Quiz 1

1. **In the beginning of "A Modest Proposal," what are the mothers of Ireland doing instead of working?**
   A. begging for their infant children
   B. stealing
   C. ignoring their infant children
   D. engaging in prostitution

2. **What do the children of the begging mothers do when they grow up?**
   A. find employment to support themselves
   B. steal, fight for Spain, or sell themselves
   C. steal, fight for France, or sell themselves
   D. borrow money to support themselves

3. **The writer calls the condition of the poor children in Ireland what?**
   A. deplorable
   B. commendable
   C. unavoidable
   D. regrettable

4. **What should be done for the person who can solve the conditions in Ireland, or "whoever could find out a fair, cheap, and easy method of making these children sound, useful members of the commonwealth"?**
   A. he should be banished
   B. he should be executed
   C. he should receive a medal
   D. a statue should be erected for him

5. **According to Swift's narrator, for how long may a child be supported on mother's milk, and perhaps two shillings?**
   A. one year
   B. two years
   C. six months
   D. three years

6. **What is NOT an advantage to his idea that Swift's narrator cites in "A Modest Proposal"?**
   A. it will decrease sibling rivalry
   B. it will decrease the population of Ireland
   C. it will decrease wife-beating
   D. it will decrease the number of voluntary abortions

7. **According to Swift's narrator, how many people live in Ireland?**
    A. one million and a half
    B. one million and a quarter
    C. one million
    D. two million

8. **At what age does the narrator in "A Modest Proposal" think children learn the ability to steal?**
    A. age one
    B. age six
    C. age three
    D. age seven

9. **The merchants assure the narrator of "A Modest Proposal" that**
    A. a child of twelve is a saleable commodity
    B. a child of twelve is not old enough to steal
    C. a child of twelve is not a saleable commodity
    D. a child of twelve would make a delicious dinner

10. **The acquaintance of the narrator, who assures him that a child is a "delicious food," is from where?**
    A. America
    B. England
    C. Formosa
    D. Spain

11. **How many females should be kept alive for "breeding" purposes, in relation to one male?**
    A. six females to one male
    B. two females to one male
    C. four females to one male
    D. three females to one male

12. **How many dishes will a child make for "entertainment for friends"?**
    A. one dish
    B. two dishes
    C. four dishes
    D. three dishes

13. **How much does Swift's narrator guess a child weighs after it is born?**
    A. twenty-eight pounds
    B. twelve pounds
    C. twenty pounds
    D. ten pounds

14. **For whom will the food of infants be "proper," as they have "already devoured most of the parents"?**
    A. the landlords
    B. the beggars
    C. the papists
    D. the priests

15. **For how long does Swift's narrator predict infant flesh will be in season?**
    A. throughout the year
    B. only in February
    C. only in the spring
    D. only in March

16. **In what month will the infants be most plentiful?**
    A. October
    B. February
    C. March
    D. April

17. **Why will the infants be most plentiful at that time?**
    A. it is nine months after Christmas
    B. it is a quirk of Irish genetics
    C. it is nine months after the end of Lent
    D. unborn children are most likely to survive to birth in that month

18. **About how much does Swift's narrator guess a gentleman will pay for the carcass of an infant?**
    A. ten shillings
    B. two shillings
    C. one pound
    D. eight shillings

19. **The carcass of an infant may serve what purposes?**
    A. ladiesâ— gloves and gentlemenâ— s hats
    B. ladiesâ— gloves and gentlemenâ— s boots
    C. gentlemenâ— s gloves and ladiesâ— boots
    D. ladiesâ— hats and gentlemenâ— s boots

20. **Who suggests to Swift's narrator that the people of Ireland also consume children of fourteen?**
    A. a very wicked person
    B. a very worthy person
    C. a priest
    D. a Spaniard

21. **Why does Swift's narrator reject the idea of eating Irish children of fourteen?**
    A. the flesh of boys of fourteen is too lean from constant exercise
    B. children of fourteen may resist capture and murder
    C. it is wrong to eat children of fourteen
    D. the flesh of boys of fourteen is too supple from constant exercise

22. **The acquaintance of the narrator has learned about cannibalism of older children from another acquaintance from where?**
    A. America
    B. Formosa
    C. Australia
    D. Spain

23. **What is the first reason Swift's narrator provides in favor of his proposal?**
    A. it will decrease wife-beating
    B. it will decrease the number of Protestants
    C. it will decrease the number of papists
    D. it will decrease the number of Puritans

24. **What is the second reason Swift's narrator provides in favor of his proposal?**
    A. it will decrease wife-beating
    B. it will decrease the number of papists
    C. it will decrease the number of Puritans
    D. it will give the poor something valuable of their own

25. **What is the third reason Swift's narrator provides in favor of his proposal?**
    A. it will decrease the overall wealth of the nation
    B. it will increase the overall wealth of the nation
    C. it will decrease the number of papists
    D. it will give the poor something valuable of their own

Quiz 1 Answer Key

1. **(A)** begging for their infant children
2. **(B)** steal, fight for Spain, or sell themselves
3. **(A)** deplorable
4. **(D)** a statue should be erected for him
5. **(A)** one year
6. **(A)** it will decrease sibling rivalry
7. **(A)** one million and a half
8. **(B)** age six
9. **(C)** a child of twelve is not a saleable commodity
10. **(A)** America
11. **(C)** four females to one male
12. **(B)** two dishes
13. **(B)** twelve pounds
14. **(A)** the landlords
15. **(A)** throughout the year
16. **(C)** March
17. **(C)** it is nine months after the end of Lent
18. **(A)** ten shillings
19. **(B)** ladies' gloves and gentlemen's boots
20. **(B)** a very worthy person
21. **(A)** the flesh of boys of fourteen is too lean from constant exercise
22. **(B)** Formosa
23. **(C)** it will decrease the number of papists
24. **(D)** it will give the poor something valuable of their own
25. **(B)** it will increase the overall wealth of the nation

Quiz 2

1. **What is the fourth reason Swift's narrator provides in favor of his proposal?**
   A. it will increase the overall wealth of the nation
   B. mothers will be free of the responsibility of raising their children
   C. it will increase the number of papists
   D. it will give the poor something valuable of their own

2. **What is the fifth reason Swift's narrator provides in favor of his proposal?**
   A. it will decrease the number of papists
   B. this new type of food will become a custom at taverns
   C. this new type of food will become a custom in churches
   D. it will give the poor something valuable of their own

3. **What is the sixth reason Swift's narrator provides in favor of his proposal?**
   A. it will bolster the institution of marriage
   B. it will decrease the number of papists
   C. it will bolster the institution of the church
   D. it will give the poor something valuable of their own

4. **What is the one objection that Swift's narrator identifies to his "modest proposal"?**
   A. it is wrong to kill and eat children
   B. infant flesh may not be appetizing
   C. it will decrease the population of Ireland
   D. it will increase the population of Ireland

5. **Swift's narrator says his proposal will not "disoblige" which country, because infant flesh cannot be exported?**
   A. America
   B. England
   C. Formosa
   D. Spain

6. **In his concluding paragraph of "A Modest Proposal," what does Swift's narrator say is his chief motive?**
   A. increasing the population
   B. the public good of his country
   C. the public good of America
   D. decreasing the number of papists

7. **In his concluding paragraph, why does Swift's narrator say he has nothing to gain personally from his proposal?**
    A. because he has no children that he could sell to be eaten
    B. because he has no wife
    C. because he is not Irish
    D. because he would never sell or eat his own children

8. **"A Modest Proposal" is an example of what genre?**
    A. satire
    B. letter
    C. treatise
    D. policy proposal

9. **In "A Modest Proposal," who are the "papists"?**
    A. Roman Catholics
    B. Puritans
    C. Popes
    D. Protestants

10. **When "A Modest Proposal" was first published, who was the author listed?**
    A. no author; it was published anonymously
    B. â— a very worthy personâ—
    C. Jonathan Swift
    D. an American acquaintance of the bookseller

11. **In what year was "A Modest Proposal" published?**
    A. 1629
    B. 1706
    C. 1729
    D. 1730

12. **When Swift's narrator lists the reasons for his proposal in "A Modest Proposal," how many reasons does he give?**
    A. one
    B. six
    C. two
    D. five

13. **Which of the following is a reason Swift gives in favor of his proposal?**
    A. it will encourage mothers to take better care of their infants
    B. it will increase poverty in Ireland
    C. it will increase the population of Ireland
    D. it will make the population of Ireland stay constant

14. **Swift's narrator says his American acquaintance assured him that infant flesh was not only delicious, but**
    A. delightful
    B. disgusting
    C. nourishing
    D. sweet

15. **According to Swift's proposal, will all of the poor Irish infants be used for food?**
    A. no, some will be kept alive as slaves
    B. no, some will be kept alive as breeders
    C. yes
    D. no, some will be kept alive to be educated

16. **Swift's proposal applies to the "poor people" of what country?**
    A. America
    B. England
    C. Ireland
    D. Scotland

17. **Swift's narrator says that some "scrupulous people" might complain "unjustly" that his friend's idea of eating fourteen-year-olds is**
    A. wise
    B. remarkable
    C. outlandish
    D. cruel

18. **For how long had Swift's narrator been "wearied" with "offering vain, idle, visionary thoughts," before coming upon his proposal?**
    A. for a couple of years
    B. for many years
    C. for a day or two
    D. for a month

19. **The acquaintance of Swift's narrator who proposes that the Irish eat children of fourteen as well received this idea from which person?**
   A. the inhabitants of Topinamboo
   B. an American
   C. Laplanders
   D. Psalmanazar

20. **According to Swift's narrator, what will the infants' parents opinion be of his proposal?**
   A. they will be confused
   B. they will be horrified
   C. they will be indifferent
   D. they will be happy not to provide for their children

21. **Swift's narrator calls the poor Irish a "breed." What effect does this have?**
   A. it dehumanizes them
   B. it has no effect
   C. it makes them appear noble
   D. it makes the reader sympathetic to them

22. **When Swift's narrator says that the Irish should eat their babies in "A Modest Proposal," he is being what on Swift's behalf?**
   A. tragic
   B. unsure
   C. serious
   D. satirical

23. **What person is "A Modest Proposal" written in?**
   A. the third person
   B. the first person
   C. the third person plural
   D. the second person

24. **What century was a "A Modest Proposal" written in?**
   A. the sixteenth century
   B. the eighteenth century
   C. the nineteenth century
   D. the seventeenth century

25. **"A Modest Proposal" expresses prejudices against which religion?**
    A. Protestantism
    B. Roman Catholicism
    C. Puritanism
    D. Anglicanism

Quiz 2 Answer Key

1. **(B)** mothers will be free of the responsibility of raising their children
2. **(B)** this new type of food will become a custom at taverns
3. **(A)** it will bolster the institution of marriage
4. **(C)** it will decrease the population of Ireland
5. **(B)** England
6. **(B)** the public good of his country
7. **(A)** because he has no children that he could sell to be eaten
8. **(A)** satire
9. **(A)** Roman Catholics
10. **(A)** no author; it was published anonymously
11. **(C)** 1729
12. **(B)** six
13. **(A)** it will encourage mothers to take better care of their infants
14. **(C)** nourishing
15. **(B)** no, some will be kept alive as breeders
16. **(C)** Ireland
17. **(D)** cruel
18. **(B)** for many years
19. **(D)** Psalmanazar
20. **(D)** they will be happy not to provide for their children
21. **(A)** it dehumanizes them
22. **(D)** satirical
23. **(B)** the first person
24. **(B)** the eighteenth century
25. **(B)** Roman Catholicism

Quiz 3

1. **According to Swift's narrator, who are the "chief breeders" of the British empire?**
   A. the English Catholics
   B. the Irish Protestants
   C. the English Protestants
   D. the Irish Catholics

2. **Who does Swift's narrator mean when he refers to "popish infants"?**
   A. The babies of the Pope
   B. English babies
   C. Irish Catholic babies
   D. Protestant babies

3. **How many Irish Catholic babies are born for every English Anglican baby, according to Swift's narrator?**
   A. one
   B. two
   C. four
   D. three

4. **Swift's narrator says the poverty-stricken conditions of what country are "deplorable"?**
   A. America
   B. England
   C. Ireland
   D. Spain

5. **Which is NOT a reason that the very young Irish children are in a sad state?**
   A. they have not yet learned to steal
   B. their mothers and fathers are unable to provide for them
   C. they fall asleep at work
   D. they are not a "saleable commodity"

6. **Which children will be consumed, according to Swift's narrator?**
   A. rich children
   B. sick children
   C. poor children
   D. fat children

7. **In the beginning of his essay, Swift's narrator assures readers that his proposal will concern more than just the children of which group (that he has described in the opening)?**
   A. priests
   B. landlords
   C. innkeepers
   D. professed beggars

8. **Who is the narrator of "A Modest Proposal"?**
   A. Jonathan Swift
   B. an anonymous Spaniard
   C. an anonymous Englishman
   D. an anonymous Englishman who has no prejudices

9. **To what degree does Jonathan Swift the writer agree with the plain argument presented by the narrator of "A Modest Proposal"?**
   A. Jonathan Swift is indistinguishable from the narrator
   B. to a fairly high degree
   C. virtually to no degree
   D. about half and half

10. **The mathematics present in "A Modest Proposal" mock which new tendency in modern thought?**
    A. the tendency to apply political ideals to social questions
    B. the tendency to apply scientific advancements to social questions
    C. the tendency to apply social advancements to scientific questions
    D. the tendency of the Irish to eat their babies

11. **Jonathan Swift wrote "A Modest Proposal" to**
    A. mock the Irish for their beliefs
    B. suggest that the Irish eat their babies
    C. mock children for their poverty
    D. expose prejudices against the poor Catholics

12. **The American acquaintance of Swift's narrator assures him that an infant of one year is not only nourishing but**
    A. adorable
    B. delicious
    C. repulsive
    D. salty

13. **In the first sentence of "A Modest Proposal," Swift's narrator says that the majority of beggars are of what sex?**
    A. the female sex
    B. either sex
    C. the young who have not come to understand sex
    D. the male sex

14. **According to Swift's narrator, what do the poor Irish "demand" in the streets?**
    A. our food
    B. our charity
    C. our understanding
    D. our children

15. **Swift's narrator subtracts, from the total number of poor "breeders" in the kingdom, which group of people?**
    A. mothers without husbands
    B. mothers who are wise
    C. mothers who miscarry or whose children die from other causes
    D. mothers who steal

16. **What does Jonathan Swift suggest the nation of Ireland do with its infant children of poor parents?**
    A. raise them to be productive members of society
    B. eat them
    C. bury them
    D. put them up for adoption by richer families

17. **Which of the following is NOT a reason Swift's narrator provides for why his proposal will support the institution of marriage?**
    A. husbands will no longer beat their wives
    B. husbands would show greater tenderness towards their wives
    C. rich men will want to marry poor women
    D. mothers will take better care of their babies

18. **In "Tale of a Tub," Peter represents which branch of Christianity?**
    A. The Church of England
    B. Greek Orthodoxy
    C. Roman Catholicism
    D. dissenting Protestants

19. **In "Tale of a Tub," Jack represents which branch of Christianity?**
    A. The Church of England
    B. Greek Orthodoxy
    C. Roman Catholicism
    D. dissenting Protestant denominations

20. **In "Tale of a Tub," Martin represents which branch of Christianity?**
    A. The Church of England
    B. Greek Orthodoxy
    C. Roman Catholicism
    D. dissenting Protestant denominations

21. **In "Tale of a Tub," the three brothers represent what?**
    A. The three kings of England, France, and Spain
    B. Three British saints
    C. The Holy Trinity
    D. Three branches of Western Christianity

22. **In what year was "A Tale of a Tub" published?**
    A. 1604
    B. 1704
    C. 1729
    D. 1753

23. **What is the purpose of the digressions in "Tale of a Tub"?**
    A. to provide plot information
    B. to answer readers' questions
    C. literary parody
    D. to reveal character information

24. **In "Tale of a Tub," what or whom does the three brothers' father represent?**
    A. The Muse
    B. Justice
    C. God
    D. Satan

25. **In "Tale of a Tub," what do the coats each of the three brothers receives represent?**
    A. their father's love for them
    B. their failure to reform
    C. their respective Bibles and religious traditions
    D. their ambition to succeed

Quiz 3 Answer Key

1. **(D)** the Irish Catholics
2. **(C)** Irish Catholic babies
3. **(D)** three
4. **(C)** Ireland
5. **(C)** they fall asleep at work
6. **(C)** poor children
7. **(D)** professed beggars
8. **(C)** an anonymous Englishman
9. **(C)** virtually to no degree
10. **(B)** the tendency to apply scientific advancements to social questions
11. **(D)** expose prejudices against the poor Catholics
12. **(B)** delicious
13. **(A)** the female sex
14. **(B)** our charity
15. **(C)** mothers who miscarry or whose children die from other causes
16. **(B)** eat them
17. **(C)** rich men will want to marry poor women
18. **(C)** Roman Catholicism
19. **(D)** dissenting Protestant denominations
20. **(A)** The Church of England
21. **(D)** Three branches of Western Christianity
22. **(B)** 1704
23. **(C)** literary parody
24. **(C)** God
25. **(C)** their respective Bibles and religious traditions

Quiz 4

1. **What do the three sons do with their coats?**
    A. bury them
    B. alter them
    C. steal them
    D. throw them up into the air

2. **What happens to the story after "A Digression Concerning Madness"?**
    A. All subsequent sections are digressions, even if they are not called digressions
    B. All subsequent sections include the allegory of the spider and the bee
    C. All subsequent sections are in French
    D. All subsequent sections continue the story of the three brothers

3. **In "The Battle of the Books," what two groups are at war?**
    A. the Protestants and the Catholics
    B. the Philosophers and the Mathematicians
    C. the Ancients and the Moderns
    D. the Poets and the Translators

4. **The spider represents which side?**
    A. the Poets
    B. the Philosophers
    C. the Moderns
    D. the Ancients

5. **The bee represents which side?**
    A. the Musicians
    B. the Philosophers
    C. the Moderns
    D. the Ancients

6. **Who wins the battle?**
    A. none of the gods knows
    B. the Moderns
    C. we don't know
    D. the Ancients

7. **What do the other books do when the spider and the bee argue in "The Battle of the Books"?**
   A. look on with interest
   B. read aloud to one another
   C. fight their most bitter battles
   D. stay on their shelves patiently

8. **In "An Argument Against Abolishing Christianity," the writer is making the argument that abolishing Christianity is akin to what political action?**
   A. the adoption of the Test Act
   B. the murder of infant children
   C. The repeal of the Test Act
   D. the banishment of the Catholics

9. **Who is the apparent writer in "An Argument Against Abolishing Christianity?"**
   A. an anonymous, rich, foppish fellow
   B. a Spanish king
   C. an American merchant
   D. Jonathan Swift

10. **In "A True and Faithful Narrative," who predicts that a comet will strike the earth?**
    A. Mr. Tellington
    B. Mr. Swift
    C. Mr. Winton
    D. Mr. Whiston

11. **Where does he predict that a comet will strike?**
    A. the Great Hall
    B. the Royal Palace
    C. Main Street
    D. the Royal Exchange

12. **Under what conditions is the prediction made?**
    A. during a club meeting
    B. during a lecture
    C. during a political debate
    D. during a literary reading

13. **When is the comet predicted to strike?**
    A. next Wednesday
    B. this Friday
    C. next Friday
    D. next Tuesday

14. **How long does it take for news of the impending strike to spread through the city?**
    A. four days
    B. two or three days
    C. two or three hours
    D. two or three months

15. **When was "A True and Faithful Narrative" published?**
    A. 1653
    B. 1704
    C. 1723
    D. 1732

16. **What do the inhabitants of the town do in "A True and Faithful Narrative" when the comet doesn't strike?**
    A. return to sin
    B. move to a different town
    C. remember those they truly love
    D. reform their lives

17. **When was "A Meditation Upon a Broomstick" published?**
    A. 1650
    B. 1704
    C. 1710
    D. 1729

18. **Which writer was Swift mocking most clearly with "A Meditation Upon a Broomstick"?**
    A. Alexander Pope
    B. Tom Worth
    C. Branwell Bronte
    D. Robert Boyle

19. **What book, most specifically, was Swift parodying with "A Meditation Upon a Broomstick"?**
    A. Temporary Reflections upon a Few Subjects
    B. A History of Ears
    C. Gulliverâ— s Travels
    D. Occasional Reflections upon Several Subjects

20. **In "A Meditation Upon a Broomstick," Swift considers whether a broomstick is like what?**
    A. a slave
    B. a man
    C. a comb
    D. a bush

21. **In "Tale of a Tub," what is so special about the coats the father gives to his three sons?**
    A. they are the first coats ever made
    B. they will be good forever, stretching and adapting to the wearer
    C. they belonged to their mother
    D. they are made of gold

22. **What does the father request of his three sons in "Tale of a Tub?"**
    A. that they sing to him
    B. that they identify who loves him most
    C. that live together as brethren
    D. that they fight for their honor

23. **In "A Tale of a Tub," the three brothers fall in love with three women representing which vices?**
    A. Covetousness, Lust, and Pride
    B. Sloth, Covetousness, and Pride
    C. Ambition, Pride, and Sloth
    D. Covetousness, Ambition, and Pride

Quiz 4 Answer Key

1. **(B)** alter them
2. **(A)** All subsequent sections are digressions, even if they are not called digressions
3. **(C)** the Ancients and the Moderns
4. **(C)** the Moderns
5. **(D)** the Ancients
6. **(C)** we don't know
7. **(A)** look on with interest
8. **(C)** The repeal of the Test Act
9. **(A)** an anonymous, rich, foppish fellow
10. **(D)** Mr. Whiston
11. **(D)** the Royal Exchange
12. **(B)** during a lecture
13. **(C)** next Friday
14. **(C)** two or three hours
15. **(D)** 1732
16. **(A)** return to sin
17. **(C)** 1710
18. **(D)** Robert Boyle
19. **(D)** Occasional Reflections upon Several Subjects
20. **(B)** a man
21. **(B)** they will be good forever, stretching and adapting to the wearer
22. **(C)** that live together as brethren
23. **(D)** Covetousness, Ambition, and Pride

ClassicNotes

Gr▲deSaver™

Getting you the grade since 1999™

Other ClassicNotes from GradeSaver™

1984
Absalom, Absalom
Adam Bede
The Adventures of Augie March
The Adventures of Huckleberry Finn
The Adventures of Tom Sawyer
The Aeneid
Agamemnon
The Age of Innocence
The Alchemist (Coelho)
The Alchemist (Jonson)
Alice in Wonderland
All My Sons
All Quiet on the Western Front
All the King's Men
All the Pretty Horses
Allen Ginsberg's Poetry
The Ambassadors
American Beauty
Angela's Ashes
Animal Farm
Anna Karenina
Anthem
Antigone
Antony and Cleopatra
Aristotle's Ethics
Aristotle's Poetics
Aristotle's Politics
As I Lay Dying
As You Like It
Astrophil and Stella
Atlas Shrugged

The Awakening
Babbitt
The Bacchae
Bartleby the Scrivener
The Bean Trees
The Bell Jar
Beloved
Benito Cereno
Beowulf
Bhagavad-Gita
Billy Budd
Black Boy
Bleak House
Bless Me, Ultima
Blindness
The Bloody Chamber
Bluest Eye
The Bonfire of the Vanities
The Book of the Duchess and Other Poems
The Book Thief
Brave New World
Breakfast at Tiffany's
Breakfast of Champions
The Brothers Karamazov
The Burning Plain and Other Stories
A Burnt-Out Case
By Night in Chile
Call of the Wild
Candide
The Canterbury Tales
Cat on a Hot Tin Roof
Cat's Cradle
Catch-22

The Catcher in the Rye
The Caucasian Chalk Circle
Charlotte's Web
The Cherry Orchard
The Chocolate War
The Chosen
A Christmas Carol
Christopher Marlowe's Poems
Chronicle of a Death Foretold
Civil Disobedience
Civilization and Its Discontents
A Clockwork Orange
The Color of Water
The Color Purple
Comedy of Errors
Communist Manifesto
A Confederacy of Dunces
Confessions
Connecticut Yankee in King Arthur's Court
The Consolation of Philosophy
Coriolanus
The Count of Monte Cristo
Crime and Punishment
The Crucible
Cry, the Beloved Country
The Crying of Lot 49
Cymbeline

For our full list of over 250 Study Guides, Quizzes,
Sample College Application Essays, Literature Essays and E-texts, visit:

www.gradesaver.com

ClassicNotes

GrAdeSaver™

Getting you the grade since 1999™

Other ClassicNotes from GradeSaver™

Daisy Miller
David Copperfield
Death in Venice
Death of a Salesman
The Death of Ivan Ilych
Democracy in America
Devil in a Blue Dress
Dharma Bums
The Diary of a Young
   Girl by Anne Frank
Disgrace
Divine Comedy-I:
   Inferno
Do Androids Dream of
   Electric Sheep?
Doctor Faustus
   (Marlowe)
A Doll's House
Don Quixote Book I
Don Quixote Book II
Dora: An Analysis of a
   Case of Hysteria
Dr. Jekyll and Mr. Hyde
Dracula
Dubliners
East of Eden
Electra by Sophocles
The Electric Kool-Aid
   Acid Test
Emily Dickinson's
   Collected Poems
Emma
Ender's Game
Endgame
The English Patient
Ethan Frome

The Eumenides
Everything is Illuminated
Fahrenheit 451
The Fall of the House of
   Usher
A Farewell to Arms
The Federalist Papers
For Whom the Bell Tolls
The Fountainhead
Frankenstein
Franny and Zooey
The Giver
The Glass Menagerie
The God of Small Things
Goethe's Faust
The Good Earth
The Grapes of Wrath
Great Expectations
The Great Gatsby
The Guest
Gulliver's Travels
Hamlet
The Handmaid's Tale
Hard Times
Harry Potter and the
   Philosopher's Stone
Heart of Darkness
Hedda Gabler
Henry IV (Pirandello)
Henry IV Part 1
Henry IV Part 2
Henry V
Herzog
The Hobbit
Homo Faber
House of Mirth

The House of the Seven
   Gables
The House of the Spirits
House on Mango Street
Howards End
A Hunger Artist
I Know Why the Caged
   Bird Sings
I, Claudius
An Ideal Husband
Iliad
The Importance of Being
   Earnest
In Cold Blood
In Our Time
In the Time of the
   Butterflies
Inherit the Wind
An Inspector Calls
Into the Wild
Invisible Man
The Island of Dr. Moreau
Jane Eyre
Jazz
The Jew of Malta
The Joy Luck Club
Julius Caesar
Jungle of Cities
Kama Sutra
Kate Chopin's Short
   Stories
Kidnapped
King Lear
The Kite Runner
Last of the Mohicans

For our full list of over 250 Study Guides, Quizzes,
Sample College Application Essays, Literature Essays and E-texts, visit:

www.gradesaver.com

ClassicNotes

GrAdeSaver™

Getting you the grade since 1999™

Other ClassicNotes from GradeSaver™

The Legend of Sleepy Hollow
Leviathan
Libation Bearers
Life is Beautiful
Life of Pi
Light In August
The Lion, the Witch and the Wardrobe
Lolita
Long Day's Journey Into Night
Lord Jim
Lord of the Flies
The Lord of the Rings: The Fellowship of the Ring
The Lord of the Rings: The Return of the King
The Lord of the Rings: The Two Towers
A Lost Lady
The Lottery and Other Stories
Love in the Time of Cholera
The Love Song of J. Alfred Prufrock
Lucy
Macbeth
Madame Bovary
Maggie: A Girl of the Streets and Other Stories
Manhattan Transfer

Mansfield Park
The Master and Margarita
MAUS
The Mayor of Casterbridge
Measure for Measure
Medea
Merchant of Venice
Metamorphoses
The Metamorphosis
Middlemarch
A Midsummer Night's Dream
Moby Dick
A Modest Proposal and Other Satires
Moll Flanders
Mother Courage and Her Children
Mrs. Dalloway
Much Ado About Nothing
My Antonia
Mythology
Native Son
Nickel and Dimed: On (Not) Getting By in America
Night
Nine Stories
No Exit
Notes from Underground
O Pioneers
The Odyssey

Oedipus Rex or Oedipus the King
Of Mice and Men
The Old Man and the Sea
Oliver Twist
On Liberty
On the Road
One Day in the Life of Ivan Denisovich
One Flew Over the Cuckoo's Nest
One Hundred Years of Solitude
Oroonoko
Othello
Our Town
The Outsiders
Pale Fire
Paradise Lost
A Passage to India
The Pearl
Perfume: The Story of a Murderer
Persuasion
Phaedra
Phaedrus
The Piano Lesson
The Picture of Dorian Gray
Poe's Poetry
Poe's Short Stories
Poems of W.B. Yeats: The Rose
Poems of W.B. Yeats: The Tower

For our full list of over 250 Study Guides, Quizzes,
Sample College Application Essays, Literature Essays and E-texts, visit:

www.gradesaver.com

ClassicNotes

GrAdeSaver™

Getting you the grade since 1999™

Other ClassicNotes from GradeSaver™

The Poetry of Robert
  Frost
The Poisonwood Bible
Portrait of the Artist as a
  Young Man
Pride and Prejudice
The Prince
Prometheus Bound
Pudd'nhead Wilson
Pygmalion
Rabbit, Run
A Raisin in the Sun
The Real Life of
  Sebastian Knight
The Red Badge of
  Courage
The Remains of the Day
The Republic
Rhinoceros
Richard II
Richard III
The Rime of the Ancient
  Mariner
Rip Van Winkle and
  Other Stories
The Road
Robinson Crusoe
Roll of Thunder, Hear
  My Cry
Romeo and Juliet
A Room of One's Own
A Room With a View
A Rose For Emily and
  Other Short Stories

Rosencrantz and
  Guildenstern Are
  Dead
Salome
The Scarlet Letter
The Scarlet Pimpernel
The Seagull
The Secret Life of Bees
Secret Sharer
Sense and Sensibility
A Separate Peace
Shakespeare's Sonnets
Shantaram
Siddhartha
Silas Marner
Sir Gawain and the
  Green Knight
Sister Carrie
Six Characters in Search
  of an Author
Slaughterhouse Five
Snow Falling on Cedars
The Social Contract
Something Wicked This
  Way Comes
Song of Roland
Song of Solomon
Sons and Lovers
The Sorrows of Young
  Werther
The Sound and the Fury
The Spanish Tragedy
Spring Awakening
The Stranger
A Streetcar Named
  Desire

The Sun Also Rises
Tale of Two Cities
The Taming of the Shrew
The Tempest
Tender is the Night
Tess of the D'Urbervilles
Their Eyes Were
  Watching God
Things Fall Apart
The Things They Carried
A Thousand Splendid
  Suns
The Threepenny Opera
Thus Spoke Zarathustra
The Time Machine
Titus Andronicus
To Build a Fire
To Kill a Mockingbird
To the Lighthouse
Treasure Island
Trifles
Troilus and Cressida
Tropic of Cancer
Tropic of Capricorn
The Turn of the Screw
Twelfth Night
Twilight
Ulysses
Uncle Tom's Cabin
Utopia
A Very Old Man With
  Enormous Wings
Villette
The Visit
Volpone
Waiting for Godot

For our full list of over 250 Study Guides, Quizzes,
Sample College Application Essays, Literature Essays and E-texts, visit:

www.gradesaver.com

ClassicNotes

GrAdeSaver™

Getting you the grade since 1999™

Other ClassicNotes from GradeSaver™

For our full list of over 250 Study Guides, Quizzes,
Sample College Application Essays, Literature Essays and E-texts, visit:

www.gradesaver.com

Made in the USA
Lexington, KY
30 September 2012